ALL I REALLY
NEED TO KNOW
IN BUSINESS
I LEARNED
AT MICROSOFT

ALL I REALLY NEED TO KNOW IN BUSINESS I LEARNED AT MICROSOFT

INSIDER STRATEGIES TO HELP YOU SUCCEED

Julie Bick

POCKET BOOKS

New York   London   Toronto   Sydney   Tokyo   Singapore

POCKET BOOKS, a division of Simon & Schuster Inc.
1230 Avenue of the Americas, New York, NY 10020

ISBN: 0-671-00913-3

First Pocket Books hardcover printing July 1997

10   9   8   7   6   5   4   3   2

POCKET and colophon are registered trademarks of
Simon & Schuster Inc.

Printed in the U.S.A.

For Rogers

ACKNOWLEDGMENTS

Thanks to Microsofties who lent me their wit and wisdom both on the job and for the book: Craig Bartholomew, Judy Chase, Bettijean Collins, Michel Girard, Jon DeVaan, Stephanie Libresco DeVaan, Melinda French, Charlotte Guyman, Pete Higgins, Tom Jaffee, Ruthann Lorentzen, Chris Peters, Jeff Raikes, Russ Siegelman, Kathleen Schoenfelder, Ron Souza, Marty Taucher, David Thatcher, Hank Vigil, Ben Waldman, and Susan Weeber.

And to those who helped make this happen: Amy Einhorn, Dan Greenberg, Greer Kessel, and Jon Karp, who started the ball rolling. And Neal Gantcher who helped me as a friend of the family, even though it wasn't my family he's a friend of!

Thanks also to my uncle, Don Franklin, for the book's inspiration and Dean Hachamovitch, a wealth of stories, joke E-mails, and the inventor of my favorite Word for Windows feature, "autocorrect." And to my parents for their endless support.

CONTENTS

ALL I REALLY
NEED TO KNOW
IN BUSINESS
I LEARNED
AT MICROSOFT

INTRODUCTION

If you're like me, you usually skip the introductions to business books and get right to the juicy stuff. Feel free to skip this one too, but if you want to find out a bit more about why I wrote the book, and what you may get out of it, read on . . . I promise I'll make it short. And—just so you feel good about your purchase—know that I'm giving half the proceeds to charity.

Say the word *Microsoft* and it conjures up all sorts of preconceived images—from ruthless competitors to twenty-seven-year-old nerd millionaires working around the clock. In fact, Microsofties, as employees call themselves, are the people who poke the most fun at Microsoft's reputation. Here's part of an E-mail message that was forwarded around the company spoofing Microsoft's work-hard culture:

TO:	Team
FROM:	?
RE:	Burnout Prevention and Recovery: Health Tips for the '90s and Their Microsoft Counterparts

AVOID ISOLATION. Don't do everything alone! Develop or renew intimacies with friends and loved ones. Closeness not only brings new insights, but also is anathema to agitation and depression.
> MICROSOFT VIEW: Shut your office door and lock it from the inside so no one will distract you. They're just trying to hurt your productivity.

LEARN TO SAY "NO." You'll help diminish intensity by speaking up for yourself. This means refusing additional requests or demands on your time or emotions.
> MICROSOFT VIEW: Never say no to anything. It shows weakness, and lowers the stock price. Never put off until tomorrow what you can do at midnight.

REASSESS YOUR VALUES. Try to sort out the meaningful values from the temporary and fleeting, the essential from the nonessential. You'll conserve energy and time, and begin to feel more centered.
> MICROSOFT VIEW: Stop thinking about your own problems. This is selfish. If your values change, we will make an announcement at the company meeting. Until then, if someone calls you and questions your priorities, tell them that you are unable to comment on this and give them the number for Microsoft Marketing. It will be taken care of.

Say what you will about Microsoft, but it's the best training ground for anyone interested in business—any business. Experience that might take years to gain elsewhere comes in bursts of just a few weeks at Microsoft. The pace is intense, the market changes constantly, the growth is phenomenal, and yes, you even get to see CEO Bill Gates. What more could someone want? Well, actually, a lot. Like a little guidance, which is what you'll be getting in this book.

I signed on at Microsoft in 1990, a freshly minted Wharton MBA. I felt well equipped to succeed in my job, and indeed, when I started, I was excited to see that Microsoft really did use all those buzzwords I had learned at school. They had "target audiences" and "niche markets." They ran "focus groups" and calculated "ROI"—"return on investment." I cruised blithely into the world of corporate America.

Soon, however, I started noticing there were things going on that weren't covered in the classroom. Some managers were adored by their teams and revered as "stars," while others just got grumbles in response when you asked about them. Some of the E-mail, memos, and meetings were incredibly concise and focused, while others rambled on endlessly. Decisions were made, people switched groups, and I realized there were major dimensions to my job and my company that I didn't really understand. What was the real secret to making a bunch of employees into a crackerjack team? How could my product stay ahead of its competitors? How do I keep my own career moving forward? What should I do if I have a bad boss?

Friends at other companies told me they were experiencing the same things and facing similar questions. I figured I was surrounded by some premier business minds, so I set out to make Microsoft my classroom.

I began listening more closely to my peers and managers and watching what my competitors were doing. I examined my own mistakes. As I tuned in to what was happening around me, I learned how to succeed and emulated the traits of successful managers. I saw how to trade off priorities without dropping the ball, the best way to analyze a business and rival products, and how to manage expectations. As a manager, I was taught how to motivate a team, hire winners, and communicate strategy. I found mentors (that's right, you have to *find* mentors; as with the tooth fairy, you can forget about them just appearing by your side) who showed me how to think beyond my scope of responsibilities and take the right risks. In short, I found out a great deal about the personal, managerial, and organizational practices that have helped Microsoft win.

My time at Microsoft was incredibly exciting, filled with phenomenal people and fierce challenges (or was that fierce people and phenomenal challenges?). I wrote this book to pass on what I've learned to managers, entrepreneurs, new employees, and anyone who's interested in taking a look behind the scenes at one of the most successful companies in memory and applying what they learn to their own professional lives. The things I learned about doing my job—being a manager, running a business, and keeping my career on track—can be applied to any field, by anyone. So no matter what industry you're in, try these lessons out. See what happens.

And let me know what you think. E-mail me care of my publisher at julie_bick@prenhall.com.

1 ALL I REALLY NEED TO KNOW ABOUT RUNNING A BUSINESS I LEARNED AT MICROSOFT

Whether you're in charge of a small product, a set of accounts, or an entire division, the rules are the same: keep in touch with your customers, and pay attention to the ever-changing market forces so you can jump on new opportunities quickly or pull the rip cord on losing propositions. Running a successful business also means letting your employees know they can fail, every now and then, so they will be willing to take the right risks. And while it's easy to get sidetracked by competitor moves and industry fire drills, you'll do best if you keep your focus on the drive to win. Remember, if you're not winning, you can always try changing the rules.

SETTING UP TO PLAY

LESSON

1

EAT YOUR OWN DOG FOOD, BUT DON'T BELIEVE YOUR OWN PRESS RELEASES

My summer job at age sixteen was selling Godiva chocolates in the local mall. My manager there told me, "Don't just read the descriptions on the brochure, eat every kind of candy we're selling so you can describe and recommend them to customers." I happily complied. A variation of that principle is used at Microsoft. It's not quite as delightful as taste-testing truffles but serves a similar purpose.

In what is called "Eating your own dog food," Microsoft employees use test versions of all the products on a daily basis long before they come out. Windows 95 marketers used the new operating system every day for months before it was finally ready for market. Teams working on everything from Word, the word processor, to the Encarta CD-ROM encyclopedia do the same thing.

Eating your own dog food is not always pleasant. When Microsoft rolled out their new E-mail system to tens of thousands of employees, there were delays, computer crashes, lost mail, and lost productivity. In one glitch, the computer E-mail screen would freeze up for forty-five seconds and then go back to normal. One employee joked, "We thought this might be some kind of feature that prevented repetitive-stress injury on your wrists by forcing you to stop working

▼   SIMPLE CAVEMAN NEEDUM PRINTER HELP   ▲

The following E-mail was received over the Internet, and immediately sent all over Microsoft.

TO:	?
FROM:	?
RE:	Simple Caveman Needum Printer Help

Me caveman, simple folk. Want hook-up two printer, two computer.

OOG, let me scratch on cave wall:

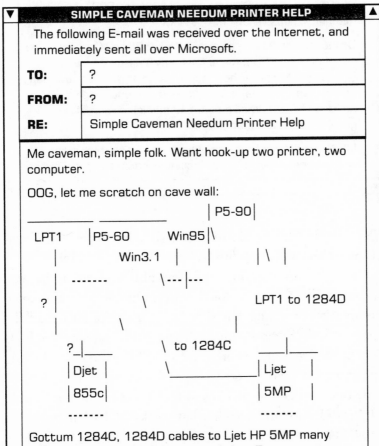

Gottum 1284C, 1284D cables to Ljet HP 5MP many moons now, work like bear-bone charm. Two computers talk to HP Ljet, share-share-alike. HP Ljet 5MP like EPP, like talk to P5-90, P5-60, say "me here! me busy! me needum paper!"

Then Djet 855c join home last moon, much powerful magic. Needum make P5-90 talkum to Djet too. Don't like way me change printers now. Gottum shut down P5-90, change cables, reboot. Win95 stink like big pile mammoth dung, many flies, much bad wind.

Me think me just add new parallel port, LPT2, on little card. But evil spirits lurk; not many IRQs, caveman afraid change soundcard IRQ from 5, for evil Win95 never saw soundcard, will kill or hurt soundcard if find out. Need LPT2 me can assign any IRQ. Me see FarPoint makum extra Parallel port card, but FarPoint say no good with evil, evil

Win95. Me want EPP port, most card not EPP, or have all manner expensive junk me no want.

Or maybe can use fast serial with HP 855c? Gottum extra serial port on 855c, made for funny fruit computer (Appletalk? Me never hear apple talk in all days as caveman, travel many many lands). Gottum extra unused 16550 serial on P5-90. Win95 bad, bad medicine. Stink like ground sloth with mange.

MS try make like fruit computer, computer think it know what caveman want, really just do random thing it want.

and take a coffee break. But after six trips to the coffee machine in one morning, I'm so hyper I can't see straight."

"Eating your own dog food" can also translate to living a scenario you've painted for the user. One of the top managers in the Consumer Division keeps a computer on all the time in her kitchen because Microsoft is designing products for the future home where the PC will be in a central living space, rather than in today's spare bedroom, where it's used only once a week to play a game or balance the checkbook. "It lets her see for herself what works and what hurts," a coworker told me.

"Eat your own dog food, but don't believe your own press releases" means use the product for yourself, rather than read about all its great features in a press release. See what it's like to be a customer and you can empathize with them, understand their needs and frustrations. Microsofties use this experience to know the product that they're developing, testing, or selling inside and out.

LESSON

2

EXAMINE YOUR MISTAKES

Microsofties relentlessly study their underdog products, failed marketing programs, and missed forecasts. This is not to assign blame or prove why it was someone else's fault. Many of the company's best lessons have come from failures. Microsofties figure as long as they lost all that money, mind share, or market share, they may as well learn something from it.

A Microsoft manager returned from a trade show and joyously sent out a piece of E-mail to his team, announcing their product had won nine out of ten possible awards. Within a day he received forty E-mails back asking which award they had not won, and why. Such is the intensity of Microsoft's focus.

After each new software product ships, a "postmortem" is held. From the Latin words meaning "after death," a postmortem analzyes what went wrong and what went well during the life of a project. People are interviewed, reports written, actions and decisions analyzed, and the results are published so any lessons learned can be disseminated around the company. The same is done informally with marketing programs as results and measurements are available. And although these reports show the warts of the team, the product, and the process, they are shared.

When a product or project doesn't meet its goals, Microsofties try to figure out why. The implementation may have been flawless, but the basic premise wrong. Such was the case with Microsoft's Trial Plus program, which gave corporations free Word and Excel software to try for ninety days.

The Trial Plus team did a crackerjack job. They screened corporate users, sent out software, followed up at prescribed times to see if their charges had installed the software, were training others, and so on. In the end they expected those who had tried Microsoft software to switch over and buy it for their whole office. What they found was a very high satisfaction level with the program and the products but a low translation to sales.

Internally, we started to call the program Piracy Plus because it seemed some of the businesses who were trying the software were just keeping it and copying it onto their network. The Trial Plus program was canceled, but the team retained its solid reputation based on their work with customers.

LESSON

3

LET PEOPLE FAIL

Personal mistakes are also more likely to be examined than punished. Microsoft vice president Jon DeVaan's words are echoed around the company. "If you fire the person who failed, you're throwing away the value of the experience."

Microsoft has a great tradition of promoting people who were in charge of failed projects. Vice President Russ Siegelman jokingly describes his career, "I worked on the marketing for LAN Manager. It was a flop. They promoted me to be in charge of marketing of Windows for Workgroups—it got off to a rocky start. I was promoted to be Bill's (Gates's) assistant, investigating the on-line business, and was put in charge of creating Microsoft's on-line service. That got off to a rocky start too and they made me a vice president. Imagine if I had been on successful products!"

When the product manager of Microsoft's spreadsheet software came to Bill Gates in 1984 and told him there was a major bug in the product and it would have to be recalled from retailers, Bill told him, "Well, you came in to work today and lost two hundred and fifty thousand dollars. Tomorrow you'll hope to do better." Today, that product manager, Jeff Raikes, is a member of Microsoft's Office of the President.

There's a company-wide commitment to accepting mistakes as part of the process because so many new areas are being explored. Allowing people to fail with impunity (on the right occasions) paves the way for those people to take risks again in the future. And the rest of the company, watching from the sidelines, will feel emboldened as well. They'll be more free with their ideas. They won't shy away from a project that has a chance of going under. The freedom to fail helps move the company forward.

The saying, "Whenever you screw up, you get promoted," has been known to come up laughingly at Microsoft meetings.

LESSON

4

SOMETIMES TANKERS CAN LOOK LIKE SPEEDBOATS

Even big, ungainly organizations can be nimble, especially if they have a clear direction and the autonomy to make the changes they need.

In May of 1995, not many people were working on things related to the Internet at Microsoft. And those who did worked in only a few of Microsoft's many divisions. Other areas, such as the multibillion dollar Word and Excel businesses, barely thought about it. What did the World Wide Web have to do with someone sitting at a desk typing a memo or adding a bunch of columns? Microsoft was planning an on-line service that connected to the Internet, but it was designed to be separate from it. Some of the CD-ROM groups were looking into playing games over a network or delivering information to customers via Microsoft's on-line service, but they weren't paying much attention to the Internet. A couple of Internet "champions" hounded Bill Gates until he saw the importance of this new area, which culminated in a single memo that changed the entire direction of the company.

Bill's May 1995 memo called, "The Internet Tidal Wave," galvanized the company from top to toe. By December, the tanker that was Microsoft had turned into hundreds of small speedboats, focused on one thing and one thing only—the Web. Within six months, every product plan and marketing strategy included an Internet component.

Turning a business on its ear isn't done just by the CEO at Microsoft; it happens at a variety of levels. The Consumer

Division had approved and was working on plans for travel CD-ROMs. This seemed like a great idea—multimedia could do so much to improve on paperbound travel books. There would be moving pictures, sound, huge hotel and restaurant listings. Itinerary planners would let you enter your interests, budget, time you'd be spending at the destination, and the CD-ROM could offer itineraries, maps, museum hours, hotel suggestions, and so on.

Rich Barton, a young product planner, joined the group to study the market and help shape the new CD-ROMs. He dove into his job, devouring all the information he could get his hands on.

After a few weeks, he appeared in his manager's office and said, "You know what? Books on traveling to England make about ten million dollars a year. But travel agents' fees on booking tickets to England add up to one hundred million!" He made a case for changing the plans from CD-ROMs to on-line travel-planning and booking services. This new twist would still take advantage of Microsoft's multimedia and technology strengths, but would bring them into a much bigger market. His managers agreed, and two years later Rich was heading up the launch of Microsoft's Internet travel planning service.

LESSON

5

LET YOUR EMPLOYEES HEAR YOUR CUSTOMERS

You can imagine or guess what your customers think of this or that product or service. But there's no replacement for asking them directly.

Here are a handful of the ways Microsofties listen to customers:

- Most marketing managers are required to spend time on the Product Support phone lines, listening to technicians trying to solve customer's software problems.
- Letters mailed to Bill Gates concerning a particular product make their way from Bill's office to the employee responsible for that product, and a response to the customer is usually expected.
- As he built Microsoft's new on-line service, the vice president in charge would sift through the thousands of E-mails he received from users and forward a variety of kudos and complaints on to his team.
- Most new products go through a test where volunteers using the software are watched through a one-way mirror by everyone from programmers to marketers to psychologists who ask, "How does that make you feel?"

The use of customer feedback has practically been made into a science in the development of new products. The first few versions of Word and Excel were pretty darn hard to use. For example, the seemingly nonsensical "Escape, Transfer, Load" was the command sequence to open up a new document in Word. Customer input wasn't well integrated with product development. The biggest problem was that the feedback came after the product was finished—rather than along the way.

By switching to a process of getting detailed customer input early, designers and programmers were able to create the right features along the way. The product-development groups sent researchers to speak to groups of customers and see what they did with their software—what they used it for and how they used it. The researchers visited top corporate customers, as well as legal firms, small businesses, schools, and other organizations.

Special versions of Word and Excel were created that recorded every single keystroke a user made. These special products were sent to volunteers around the world who didn't mind letting researchers see everything they were doing with their software. By looking at their work, the development team saw which were the most often used and least often used features. They looked at the most popular ones and put those features on the toolbar for one-click access. They looked at the least popular ones and tried to figure out whether those features weren't often needed or were too hard to find or use.

Soon after implementing these practices, Word and Excel began to pull ahead of rivals Lotus 1-2-3 and WordPerfect in product reviews. Sales started a major uptick.

Listening means including business partners too. When an executive at CompUSA, a major seller of Microsoft software, commented in a meeting, "I don't know who would make that decision at Microsoft, but I know it would take a long time," the head of the Microsoft sales force reorganized his one thousand people into specialized units, each with a clear focus and decision-making power.

6

DON'T BET AGAINST YOUR OWN TEAM'S CREATIVITY

You may be tempted to go to an outside firm for creative marketing ideas, new product names, or management tips. Before you go to these high-priced experts, give your own team a chance to do the work. They may have great ideas.

The marketing team for Office (a package of programs) wanted a cool name for a set of breakthrough software features that offered users a compelling new twist. These new features tried to figure out what the user wanted to do and then would do it. In Word, this meant automatically correcting spelling and typing errors without the user needing to run the spell checker. In Excel, this meant automatically formatting a spreadsheet so that it looked great rather than requiring the user to put in borders, shading, and fonts, one step at a time. A new help feature in all the products not only explained to users how to do a task, such as save a presentation under a new name, but at the user's request would actually do that thing for them.

Microsoft hired an expensive professional naming firm to come up with some monikers that could communicate this idea to users—that these new features figured out what you wanted to do, then did it for you, saving you lots of time and hassle. Two weeks and thousands of dollars later, the agency returned and presented their recommended name: "Plion."

The room was deadly still. Finally, one young manager held up his hand in a Vulcan greeting and said, "I am from the planet Plion." The room broke into laughter. As in the case of "Certs with Retsyn," no one knew what Plion was, but the agency figured if Microsoft put enough money behind it, it would be something folks wanted. Their second recommendation was "Friday." As in, "Excel now comes with Friday, built right in!!" Like your "man Friday." Needless to say, these names met with steely disapproval.

Meanwhile, my friend Matt, a product manager, corralled me and said, "Let's have a few beers and try to come up with a name ourselves." I agreed, and we took a six-pack out to the courtyard near our offices.

We listed the attributes we wanted the name to portray. We wrote things like, "Knows what you want to do. Does the work for you. Saves you time. Intelligence. Senses what you need." From there we started brainstorming names. Things like "Gatesware," "Timesavers," and "Intellitime" started emerging. We didn't like any of them.

"Okay, let's read down our list of attributes again," Matt suggested and took a swig of beer. He started to read off the word "Intelligence," but since he had beer in his mouth, it sounded like "Intellisense."

"That's it!" I cried. "IntelliSense! The features are *intelligent* and *sense* what you want to do. Then they do it for you." IntelliSense made sense. Our managers liked it.

And so IntelliSense started getting used in press releases, advertisements, direct mail, product demonstrations, and all communications about the new Microsoft features. For the next few years it could be found all over Microsoft communications. And Matt's and my greatest chuckle came when WordPerfect Corporation later came out with their own moniker, "PerfectSense," an obvious copy of our idea.

LESSON

7

TAILOR YOUR MESSAGE TO YOUR CUSTOMER

The same product can offer different benefits to different groups. Listen to what your customers say before you choose your message.

Microsoft marketed the earliest versions of its spreadsheet, Excel, to two target audiences in two different ways.

In 1985 the Apple Macintosh was a fledgling machine in the corporate world. Lots of corporate folks who chose the Mac over the IBM PC considered themselves trendsetters, rebels breaking the mold. Many became mini-evangelists, touting the superiority of the Mac wherever they went.

Microsoft introduced its new Excel spreadsheet for the Macintosh. The marketers looked at all the angles they could use to sell it. What were the key benefits to users? Was it a certain function or feature? Was it the look of the product or how easy it was to use?

Finally they decided to use the psychology of the Mac evangelists who wanted to prove their choice of machine was superior to the standard IBM PC. Mac Excel was compared head-to-head with Lotus 1-2-3, which ran on the IBM PC. The Excel marketers pointed out feature by feature, benefit by benefit, the advantages of Mac Excel over Lotus 1-2-3 for the IBM PC. To Mac users, their target audience, the superiority of a Macintosh piece of software over an IBM piece of software solidified and confirmed their supposition that the Apple was superior to the IBM PC. They bought Excel as proof.

Soon after, Microsoft came out with Excel for the IBM

PC. The target market this time was the Lotus 1-2-3 users themselves. Those users had built their expertise, their experience, and in some cases their careers on Lotus 1-2-3 skills. Microsoft couldn't come in comparing the two products as they had with the Mac users, pointing out Lotus's flaws. That would imply that Lotus users had made the wrong choice and would insult them. The tack this time was to tell Lotus users they had made a great decision over the years with the best product for the time. But now it was a new time and there was a new product to consider. With this message, rather than a head-to-head comparison, Lotus users didn't feel insulted for their past choice but were cajoled into thinking about a new one.

LESSON

EVERY PROCESS CAN
BE IMPROVED

Whether you're streamlining decision making, gathering customer feedback, developing new products, or just going about the things you do on a daily basis, look for ways to make things easier and automatic.

At Microsoft, one of the dull low-level tasks involved in creating software is to do "the daily build." The person doing the daily build takes all the different "code" (written programs) from the programmers and puts it on one computer, making sure it all works together. For years this was performed by an entry-level person and regarded as grunt work. One manager changed that and, in doing so, made the process more efficient.

This manager gave the daily-build responsibilities to the people writing the code. Each day all the programmers would give their code to one "buildmeister," who put it all together. If the code didn't work together, the person whose code was found to be the culprit then became the buildmeister as a punishment, until someone else's code screwed up the system. In the summer of 1996 the buildmeister was also given an enormous zucchini, which soon became known as the "zucchini of questionable freshness," sometimes with a fake nose and glasses, to keep in their office until the new buildmeister was named. The benefits of this (the new process, not the zucchini) were:

- No one wanted to be the buildmeister, so there was extra incentive to hand in quality code that didn't break the system.
- The unpleasant task was shared by everyone in the group.
- Higher level people were doing the task. They wanted to spend as little time on it as possible, so when their turn came, they tried to think of ways to automate the task of buildmeister and did so successfully.

LESSON

9

STAY SMALL

At their best, Microsoft's business units are run to think like small entrepreneurial shops but spend big marketing and research-and-development budgets. Employees who feel that they have ownership and decision-making capabilities are more likely to do their best than those who feel like cogs in the bureaucracy.

Despite the fact that Microsoft has grown tremendously, most Microsoft teams aren't any larger than they ever were. They just keep getting broken up into smaller and smaller specialties. Instead of a single team focused on the new Excel software, there are a number of "feature teams" that each focus on a certain area of the product. Together they all still strive for the same thing—the best software possible. However, the small teams' size lets their members feel as if they own a problem and can strive to solve it. They can see and feel their impact on the larger project.

Most Microsoft teams are also smaller than competitors' teams working on a similar product. In 1988 fifteen programmers worked on Microsoft's Excel, compared to a reported one hundred on Lotus's 1-2-3 software. That tendency to smallness is still true and gives Microsoft teams an underdog mentality, even if they are ahead in the market.

As Microsoft's teams and products get bigger, overspending and bureaucracy can start to creep in, so the company tries to stick to its small-team roots. When Microsoft bought Vermeer, a company making Internet software, it was faced with creating a product quickly with a skeleton crew. Micro-

soft looked hard at its goals and how it could carry them out
with so few people. Instead of adding every bell and whistle
to the new software, Microsoft just stuck to the core things
a customer would use.

Instead of building up Vermeer's teams to the spending
levels and complexity of those of mammoth Word and Excel,
Word and Excel took on the challenge to do things "The
Vermeer Way." They rethought the procedures and processes they had built up over time, and they tried to go back
to the leaner and meaner early days.

LESSON

10   ACT LIKE A LEADER

*A saying you'll hear a lot at Microsoft is "Take the high
road." It means act like a leader. Don't bash the
competition. Stay humble. Avoid being cocky. You can
still get your message across, but customers, press
people, and even the competition will respect you more
if you "take the high road."*

An example of taking the high road is the ad run for Microsoft's Excel spreadsheet in 1990. It stated, "9 out of 10
Excel users are very satisfied. What are we doing wrong?"
The ad included a form to fill out and send to Microsoft
with product suggestions. Excel got their point across, that
users were extremely happy with the product, but it did it

in a way that focused on customers and making even more improvements, rather than bragging.

When Windows 95 shipped, Apple ran expensive ads in the *Wall Street Journal* and on the sides of city buses that read, "C:\ongratultns.win95." Folks well versed in the software industry knew Apple was trying to make fun of the fact that Windows still used complicated commands and file names. However, most of America did not understand the subtle slam by rival Apple. They just saw one more group congratulating Microsoft on a new product, and Microsoft saw some free advertising.

Taking the high road also includes your personal actions. If you're at an industry conference or on a panel of speakers, be gracious when asked about the competition. It's also important to "go meet your competitors," Group Vice President Jeff Raikes advises. "Stop by their booth at the trade show. Get to know them and let them see you're a regular person." They'll be less likely to make deprecating comments if they've got a friendly face associated with your company. And you may even discover areas where you can cooperate.

WINNING THE GAME

L E S S O N

1

IF YOU CAN'T WIN– CHANGE THE RULES

"You usually can't win by doing the exact same thing as your competitor, but ten percent better," says Vice President Chris Peters. "You need to change the rules to get ahead. Offer something else."

Encarta, Microsoft's multimedia CD-ROM encyclopedia, debuted in the spring of 1993. Compton's and Grolier, the established leaders in the CD-ROM encyclopedia market, both touted better editorial content and better brand-names. Compton's ads even made fun of Microsoft's offering, comparing it to a low-cost encyclopedia you'd buy in a grocery store.

The Microsoft team knew they couldn't win by just putting a better print encyclopedia on a CD-ROM. But they also saw that the PC offered more than just print. So they focused on videos, sounds, animation—a multimedia approach. They found that people didn't want to read a fifty-page explanation of how planets orbit or how cats can land on their feet, but would be intrigued if they could see it happen before their eyes. The team also connected related topics so users could jump to an interesting offshoot with one click of the mouse.

Encarta's competitors focused on what people were doing today with their encyclopedias—looking things up—and using technology to making the process faster. Encarta focused on an emotional response rather than an intellectual one. Their videos, animation, and music kept people jumping from topic to topic, spending more and more time in the encyclopedia. They wanted people to want to lose themselves in their product discovering new things. Microsoft changed the playing field to win in the encyclopedia market, eventually dominating the CD-ROM arena and even beating print encyclopedia sales.

As the Microsofties visited software stores, press people, customers, and schools, they redefined what an encyclopedia was and how it could be used. They showed off the advantages of their videos and animations, as enhancements to the printed text and as enticements to stay longer on the PC, learning. And then they added a new twist—up-to-date information.

The newest information in print encyclopedias was often six months old or more, due to long editorial and production cycles. Even the CD-ROMs on the market had a cutoff date for new content months before the product appeared on the shelf. Microsoft created a process that let them add things just a few weeks before the product hit store shelves.

The marketers made sure to highlight the recency of a big event to sell their product. In 1994 the breakthrough Middle East peace agreement was signed two weeks before Encarta was completed. A photo and recorded speech from the event and detailed Middle East information made it into the encyclopedia and, more important, from a marketing standpoint, into all the product demonstrations Microsoft gave.

L E S S O N

2   THINK THREE MOVES AHEAD

Marketing plans, technology shifts, and price cuts are never done in a vacuum. Microsofties are taught to think about the competition, customers, and partners. How will they react? What move will they make? And how would we counter it?

When a Microsoftie thinks about lowering a product's price, that person also thinks about what his or her next move would be if a competitor responded by undercutting or matching it. If a new product looks as though it's going to be a hit, the person in charge of it may do some contingency planning in case capacity at the manufacturing plant falls short of market demand.

This rule also runs in reverse. If a competitor announces plans to cut a price, run a big promotion, or introduce a new product, don't just sit back and watch. Do something.

Shortly before Windows World (a trade show that attracted tens of thousands of people), WordPerfect announced they would unveil a new version of their word-processing software at the show. The Microsoft Word marketers knew from reading the press that this new update from WordPerfect lacked some innovative features that Word had planned for later that year. These innovations were real crowd-pleasing features—great to show off. One feature automatically corrected typing and spelling errors, and the other automatically formatted your document, making it look pretty with boldface type, bullets, and different-size lettering.

Since they knew the word-processing press corps would be out covering the new version of the then market-leader, WordPerfect, the Word marketers figured they could get some coverage for Word if they showed their own new features.

With only a few days notice, the marketers leapt into action, creating a punchy product demonstration of the new features to show in their booth and writing a press release that described Word's new features, to be sent out the day WordPerfect announced its new product.

The tactics worked. WordPerfect had to share the attention from the press and customers with Word. Press people, rather than just oohing and ahhing about WordPerfect, asked them, "Do you have autocorrect? Do you have autoformat?" which were Word's new features.

In other situations, it's sometimes good to save up ammunition just in case a competitor makes a move.

When Microsoft Excel spreadsheet sales pulled ahead of those of Lotus 1-2-3, the marketing team bided their time before making the news public. Then, when the team heard that Lotus was planning to do a press release announcing that their 1-2-3 spreadsheet had won an award, they sent out a press release the same day announcing that Excel had surpassed Lotus 1-2-3 in sales. The result? Instead of covering Lotus's award, the *Wall Street Journal* ran an article entitled "The Spreadsheet Wars Are Over" highlighting Microsoft's sales.

Thinking three moves ahead can also involve long-term planning. Microsoft was trailing the business software market in the early 1980s when it decided to bet that "point-and-click" software would beat out software where users typed in written commands. Looking at the technology, the marketplace, and customers they decided to focus on winning one business area at a time. First they decided on the type of business software (point-and-click, not typed commands); then they focused on creating that software for the Macintosh computer because it had the most point-and-click possibilities for users; then later they expanded to creating the same software for Windows. It took almost a decade to implement, but that basic set of struggling business software now makes more than four billion dollars a year for Microsoft.

LESSON

3   HIT 'EM WHERE THEY AIN'T

Microsoft has often seen that a shift to a new playing field can mean great rewards for the people who get to the new platform, paradigm, or even country first with something customers want.

In 1983 Lotus Corporation introduced its 1-2-3 spreadsheet to the market, and customers loved it. Watching Lotus's success with their spreadsheet for the IBM PC, Microsoft decided to attempt to develop a "superior solution" to that PC spreadsheet, going head-to-head with Lotus 1-2-3. That superior solution was to be Excel for the IBM PC.

A few months later, while development was going full tilt, Bill Gates and Jeff Raikes (then product manager) decided to literally change Excel for the IBM PC into Excel for the Macintosh. Gates and Raikes recognized that Lotus already "owned" the PC market. The Apple Macintosh was a new machine, and there was no existing spreadsheet that would run on it. They realized this as an opportunity for Microsoft and moved in. As users switched to a new platform (from IBM to Macintosh), there was a great market opportunity. In the first of many such moves, Microsoft went after the new platform.

Microsoft's resulting product, Excel for the Macintosh, "legitimized the Mac as a business machine," says Raikes. With a spreadsheet package available, the Macintosh was seen for the first time as a viable alternative to the IBM PC in the workplace. The program's popularity was instantaneous. Excel was "recommended over any other spreadsheet on the market," according to Raikes. Since its introduction, Excel has dominated the Mac spreadsheet market, outlasting and outselling a variety of competitors from Lotus, Borland, and other companies.

LESSON

4

YOU CAN CHANGE
YOUR IMAGE

You can change your consumer promise, your product's perception, or your company image. Just make sure that new image is compelling and believable. And use your money and message to make sure it sticks over time.

In 1990 Microsoft and operating systems were seen as dull, boring, and nonmainstream. (Okay, maybe they still are, but not as much so as then!) To launch Windows 3.0 that year, the PR and marketing folks planned a big splash, but it was to be a corporate splash, with slogans like "Windows of Opportunity," lots of technical information, and other seemingly necessary but completely unexciting information.

One week before the big launch, the team reviewed some videos shot for the event of customers, industry partners, and PC makers reacting to Windows 3.0. To the team's surprise, they noticed the word "cool" kept coming up. Without any encouragement, lots of people were actually calling the Windows operating system "cool" and talking excitedly about it.

"There's your Windows 3.0 slogan," the head of sales said. "Cool."

Vastly preferring cool and exciting to corporate and technical (those attributes would come across anyway), the team over the next seven days completely refocused the event to present this new "cool" image of Windows. "Cool" buttons were printed up and became a hot commodity among the digerati. At the launch, the speakers talked not just about corporate computing issues but about the fun games that came with Windows. One of the day's highlights was the showing of a computer graphic that morphed into an image of Bill Gates pushing his glasses up his nose and saying, "cool." They played rock music. The crowd and the press loved it.

From that first realization that people could get excited about a PC operating system, to the ensuing press release comparing Windows sales to the sales of Madonna's latest album, to the 1995 Windows commercials featuring the Rolling Stones song "Start Me Up," Microsoft has aimed its budget and message at bringing Windows into the mainstream and "cool."

LESSON

5

WIN-WIN DEALS: WHAT THEY CARE ABOUT AND WHAT YOU CARE ABOUT

Negotiating doesn't have to be a zero-sum game. Win-win is possible if you look closely at what your partner cares about and what you care about.

In 1993, old-timer Word for MS-DOS barely had a marketing budget. Still, it was Word's tenth birthday, and we wanted to get some good PR for the product. After all, it had been a leader in its day, the first word processor over the years to introduce new capabilities, ship on new platforms and in new languages around the world. Our goal was to get maximum positive PR coverage for minimum dollars.

I found a small, creative PR company called The History Factory, in Washington, D.C., who specialized in celebrating corporate birthdays. Talking with them, I discovered that this was a case where we couldn't afford to pay much but had a famous name, while they were willing to forgo some cash in order to build their client list.

The History Factory knew the Smithsonian Institution was putting together a "National Historic Software Collection," and the firm proposed that a copy of Microsoft Word 1.0 from 1983 be the first donation, accompanied by a press release. We loved the idea but had our budget problem.

Usually, PR firms charge by the hour worked, rather than by the actual results they achieve. The History Factory, however, agreed to charge us by the number of newspapers and magazines that covered the Word donation. We would pay them different amounts depending on the circulation of the publication and capped the amount. This ensured we'd get as much bang for our buck as possible and solved my budgeting problem. In turn, I agreed to be available to give recommendations if we were happy with their work and they could add Microsoft to the client list they used to win new business.

The History Factory did a great job, and we ended up with over fifty articles covering Word and the Smithsonian, including one in the Sunday *New York Times*. I happily recommended the firm to potential new clients for the next two years.

To a small agency like The History Factory, having a Fortune 100 name on their client list and an open line to a recommendation was more valuable than the usual margins they charged.

LESSON

6

TRY IT OUT IN THE
REAL WORLD

*Don't spin your wheels locked up in your office. Get
your idea, your memo, your product out in front of its
intended audience. It's okay to tell them, "This isn't
complete, but here's where it's going." See how they
react and take it from there. Incrementally attacking a
problem is often the best way to solve it.*

In the Word group, programmers joked, "First we make
something possible, then we make it easy." What they meant
was that a new capability would be added to Word for Windows, such as mail-merging letters, printing envelopes, or
adding footnotes, but until thousands of users got their
hands on it and suggested improvements that the programmers then made, it wouldn't be the most elegant of imple-
mentations. Real life beat the ivory tower every time.

Microsoft's Windows for Workgroups product focused on
computer networking issues. And indeed it alleviated some
but not all of these problems for businesses. But the decision
had been made that rather than wait until all issues could be
solved, the software would be launched, immediately helping
users with a subset of their problems and paving the way for
feedback for us on what to solve next and how to prioritize
resources based on customer needs. That learning was applied to the next version of Windows, Windows 95, which
vastly improved computer networking.

Trying things out in the real world works on a smaller
scale as well. Two marketing managers were asked to give
presentations to the one thousand sales people of the Micro-

soft sales force. The first created an outline, which he ran by his boss to make sure he was on track. He made some course corrections based on his boss's comments. Then he created a draft of the presentation and showed it to some sales managers he knew to see if he was sharing the information they'd find most useful. The presentation looked fine, they thought, but they suggested he take out some of the ancillary data and add some anecdotes to keep the crowd's attention—it would be a long day of meetings. Finally, he sent the completed presentation to the meeting's organizer to make sure it didn't duplicate the information from other teams. Of course, he got great ratings. His cohort created a presentation without feedback from anyone, knowing exactly what he wanted to get across. Unfortunately, the things he wanted to get across didn't interest the sales force, and his talk bombed.

LESSON

7

MAKE BIG BETS

Put your top minds, money, and efforts behind the projects critical to the business. Focus on doing those few things well. Scattering your efforts on a bunch of smaller efforts may not leave any one of them with enough resources and momentum to really succeed.

In the early 1990s Microsoft focused millions of dollars and some of its most talented programmers on the creation of Word and Excel for the Windows platform . . . before Windows was at all popular. Taking money and top programmers away from the current Word and Excel products was a major risk. At that time, WordPerfect and Lotus dominated their respective huge markets. Betting on a new operating system would leave Microsoft even further behind in those critical businesses if the new system did poorly. "If Windows had failed, there'd be no Microsoft today," one manager posits. "That was a pretty big bet."

In the big bet of 1995–1996, Microsoft realigned the entire company around the Internet. An Internet division was created, and the Internet had a place in just about every product plan around the company. There's still a lot of uncertainty concerning the World Wide Web, but Microsoft is clearly wagering on its success. Some proof? The company scrapped its on-line service, which served over a million people, to relaunch it as an Internet site and is investing even greater sums of money to create new technology and content to put on the Web. "Bill Gates has likened the Internet to the Gold Rush," says Director of Business Development for Internet Commerce Jeff Thiel. "It's hard to know if the real winner will be a guy who strikes a vein or the people selling the pans to the miners. But when it happens, we'll be there."

LESSON

8

BIG EVENTS MAKE GOOD DEADLINES

Whether it's an upcoming budget deadline, your big selling season, or a competitor launching a new marketing campaign, a little outside pressure can help you focus, clarify, and plan.

In the fall of 1995 the press and customers thought Microsoft lacked a strategy for the emerging Internet and risked not being a player for this important new platform. And to some degree they were right. Microsoft had no clearly articulated strategies and plans. But the company scheduled a day in December of that year as Internet Strategy Day, to introduce, explain, and present their Internet plans to a group of five hundred influential press people. This forced groups all over the company to make the hard decisions, focus on hammering out the strategy, and get concrete about future product plans.

The Microsofties knew they'd be grilled by the press on whatever they said, so they had to think through every issue and prepare rock-solid answers. It would have been easy to continue on without clear goals and plans, but with an external audience and set deadlines, the heat was on.

The day arrived, and hour after hour, presentations focused on strategy, direction, goals, issues, and plans. The turnabout from earlier criticisms was dramatic. Press coverage from that day forward focused on whether Microsoft would dominate the Internet, rather than on its failure to plan for it. And the blueprints presented on that day became the marching orders of every division in the company.

All sorts of big events can serve as good deadlines. When Microsoft scheduled Developer Day for industry partners who made add-on products for Windows, the group responsible for developer relations had to decide on and create by that day all the technology, training, and support materials that large, important group needed. Meeting holiday delivery deadlines for software stores forces CD-ROM groups to focus on finishing their new products on time. When 150 international subsidiary managers were due to fly in to headquarters, the desktop-applications group had to finish their marketing plans for the year.

LESSON

9

GIVE YOUR EMPLOYEES A PIECE OF THE PIE

Microsofties wear "golden handcuffs"—stock options that vest each year, giving them shares of the company. From the CEO to administrative assistants, all share in the fortune of Microsoft, good or bad. Great results abound for both employee and company from this arrangement.

As part owners of the company, Microsofties follow the stock price and are interested in things inside the company and in the marketplace that affect that price. Hence, they usually know a great deal more about other parts of their business than is usual for employees in other companies. My friend in the mainframe business at IBM couldn't explain what OS/2 was. At Microsoft, my group assistant knew which were our big money-making divisions, what their latest ads looked like, and could reel off recent changes in Microsoft's on-line service. For an employee, knowing more about the company translates to having better decision-making ability in his or her part of it. A marketer who knew about a strategy shift in another Microsoft division took that into account when she made plans for her own product.

As part owners, Microsofties make decisions for the good of the company and may even make waves or take on extra work to see that the right thing happens. Employees who are asked to work on projects for other divisions don't see it as helping another fiefdom; they see it as working for the company and ultimately themselves.

Microsofties will also put up with a nasty workload or a less-than-optimal job longer. They're more loyal to the company because it lets them share in its wealth. Founder Bill Gates may be a billionaire, but most of his plain old college graduate and MBA employees who have been with the company a few years have earned significantly more than most of their graduating classmates. And after all, despite all the popular New Age talk of job fulfillment, professional self-esteem, and challenging growth opportunities, most people work to make money!

2 ALL I REALLY NEED TO KNOW TO DO MY JOB WELL I LEARNED AT MICROSOFT

Everyone wants to be good at their job (at least if they're reading this book, they do!). But doing the best at your job doesn't mean just completing your tasks on time and on budget anymore. To really do standout work, you need to think about the impact of your piece of the puzzle and go beyond the scope of your responsibilities. And if something's not right—whether you're drowning under your workload or bailing out from a bad boss—sit back and figure out how to get it under control.

BECOMING AN EXPERT

LESSON

1

THE ELEVATOR TEST

Study the product or service your company provides, from the 50,000-foot view down to its minutiae. What are its strengths and weaknesses? How do customers perceive it? How does it compare to the competition? Know how to show it off.

At Microsoft, marketers and salespeople are expected to be able to convincingly explain the positioning and benefits of their product in thirty seconds. This is called the "elevator test"—that is, if you found yourself in an elevator with the CEO of a Fortune 500 company and wanted to sell him or her on your product, could you do it in the time of the elevator ride? Do it and you've proven you can boil the product down to its most compelling essence.

But knowing the product goes beyond knowing the basic features and benefits. You may need to know the product's technical aspects. One of Microsoft's more obsessed product designers likes to identify the fonts used in movie credits as they roll by on the screen. "That's New Century Schoolbook," he'll whisper to his wife in the theater. She'll usually respond with an elbow to his ribs.

When you know the features, the benefits, and how to use the product like a pro, you can use these skills in typical business settings, as well as some out-of-the-way "meetings." One marketer gave an impromptu demo of Windows

95 from his laptop as he waited for a plane at Chicago's O'Hare Airport. A crowd of twenty or so gathered around. Another marketer showed off multimedia Dinosaurs to third-graders on a class trip at a local science museum.

LESSON

2

KNOW WHO YOUR
CUSTOMERS ARE AND WHO
JUST ISN'T ONE YET

Study your customers. Who are they? What benefits do they look for in your product or service category? What need does your product fulfill? What motivates customers to buy your product and stick with you?

Eric LeVine, a Word product designer, typifies a Microsoftie on a customer-research crusade. In 1994 Eric was given the mission to help Word capture the lucrative legal word-processing market. His task was to find out how, when, and why lawyers created documents and how improvements to Word would make them switch to the Microsoft product.

He traveled to thirty-five law firms in nine cities across the United States. He teleconferenced with firms in England. He listened to hours of complaints and descriptions of cross-referencing, paragraph numbering, document comparison, and federal-court formatting from lawyers. He gathered hundreds of sample documents from law firms and analyzed them intently. The result? Eric's twenty-five-page detailed plan to improve Word for the legal market. "Word's gonna kill lawyers dead," he said. (That was a compliment.) Since then Word has indeed been adopted by a great number of legal firms.

At Microsoft, new-product plans specify target customers in great detail. User surveys are always underway to discover how people buy, why they buy, levels of consumer satisfaction, their wishes for future products. Before any corporate customer comes to Microsoft for a strategy or product presentation in the Executive Briefing Center, their sales representative completes a document that details the customer's technology environment, concerns, and history so that the presenters may better tailor their presentation to the customer's key issues.

In some cases, though, it is just as important to know about the person who is **not** your customer and why. In 1992 Microsoft made a concerted effort to study WordPerfect users. WordPerfect dominated the billion-dollar word-processing category. What did their customers like so much about their product? Why did they choose it over Microsoft's Word? Did anything frustrate them about their word processor? Could we convince them to switch to Word?

The Microsoft research discovered that WordPerfect users wanted their word processor to be easy to use. They wanted their word processor to perform the most common tasks, such as spell-checking and formatting, quickly and simply. And if they were going to switch to a new word processor, they wanted the new one to be easy to learn and to be able to read their WordPerfect files so they wouldn't have to re-type all their old documents.

The Microsoft team felt Word for Windows could fulfill these requirements. So, like Pepsi going after Coke, they created The Word Challenge, where people across the country tested the products, side by side. Then they embarked on a multimillion-dollar marketing campaign that, for the first time, directly targeted users of a competing product. The ad headlines called out, "Eight out of ten WordPerfect users prefer Word" and focused on the "hot spots" the Word team had discovered. Direct-mail pieces went to WordPerfect users. Microsoft's corporate sales force set up side-by-side comparisons at potential-customer sites. Kits were offered so people could compare the products at home. In the next six months, tens of thousands of WordPerfect users switched to Microsoft Word. From the thorough examination of an important segment of **noncustomers,** Microsoft created one of its most successful marketing programs.

L E S S O N

3 THE SWOT TEAM

If you were the competition, what would you do? Meet as if you were their strategy team and write up plans for their products. Get into the competition's shoes and their minds. Whether you are right on or totally wrong in your predictions for them, the exercise will reveal a variety of scenarios you may be faced with.

As Microsoft product managers, we often examined rivals such as Lotus or Novell, hypothesized their next moves, and came up with countermeasures using the "SWOT" analysis. SWOT stands for *s*trengths, *w*eaknesses, *o*pportunities, and *t*hreats. Strengths and weaknesses are internal factors, such as a patented technology or a large cash reserve. Opportunities and threats come from outside the company. Examples might be a loyal customer base or shifting technology. Laying out the SWOT grid, we'd examine another company's products, customers, cash flow, marketing programs, distribution channel, competitors, and management.

Sometimes we guessed right, such as when we predicted Lotus would go hard after the "working together" message for their SmartSuite office software. Other times we missed the boat completely, for example, forecasting that the WingZ spreadsheet would overtake Excel on the Macintosh, or worrying that the powerful Sun workstations would become so inexpensive they would supplant personal computers in businesses. But whether our products had ten percent market share or eighty percent market share, we took time out to "think like the competition."

Meeting as a "SWOT swat team" of four to six people, we'd list out everything we knew about the company. We'd debate for a while and see where we needed more research, breaking up the meeting to comb annual reports for financial data, review press articles for clues to future moves, or put rival products through their paces to compare to our own.

We'd reconvene with our new data and debate some more. Then we stepped into our competitor's shoes. We "became" the management team for that company and wrote a business plan for them, with objectives, product plans, and marketing ideas. We took our best guess at what our rival would do next.

For our final step, we developed a Microsoft response for each competitive scenario. The whole analysis and report was presented in person or on paper to the larger team and, often, upper management.

ANALYZING THE COMPETITION ISN'T ALWAYS SERIOUS

Excerpted from a piece of employee E-mail at Microsoft.

TO:	Mac Development Team
FROM:	Dean Hachamovitch
RE:	Suggestions for a new Apple slogan, originally known as ''The Power to Be Your Best''

The Power to Eat the Rest

The Power to Beat Your Chest

The Power to Budapest

The Power to Brush with Crest

The Power to Have a Guest

The Power to Be a Pest

The Power to Build a Nest

The Power to Need a Rest

The Power to Fail a Test

The Power to Stay and Vest

The Power to Promote Unrest

The Power to Act Like You're Blessed

The Power to Subliminally Suggest

The Power to Be a Pool of Cess

The Power to Study EST

The Power to, Like IBM, Be Overdressed

LESSON

4

KNOW THE BUSINESS INSIDE AND OUT

Know your customers, product, and competitors inside and out. Individual excellence begins when you know where to apply your smarts. Bury yourself in the business and learn the leverage points. Microsoft managers take knowing these subjects seriously.

When Jeff Raikes ran the Word business in 1989, he kept a family picture of his WordPerfect counterpart, Pete Peterson, on his desk and memorized the names and birthdays of the seven kids in the photo (and still remembers most of that information today!). He took the competition seriously and wanted the same from his team.

He expected his product managers to know market research and sales details. He would suddenly appear in someone's office and fire off staccato queries like, "How many academic-edition units of PC Word have we sold this month?" or "What's the ratio in the channel of 5¼ inch disks to 3½?"

We quickly learned to know our business inside and out. Armed with this data, we could spot trends, make better decisions in critical situations, and defend our thinking. And we could defend ourselves when Jeff entered our offices. While not all managers are as intense as Jeff, think-on-your-feet dialogues go on all the time at Microsoft, training you to know your stuff. And while you might not be called upon to know your competitor's family, intense knowledge of the business will just plain make you better at your job.

LESSON

5

KNOW THE QUESTIONS YOUR BOSS IS GOING TO ASK

It's easier to sit at your desk and poke holes in your own work, when you have time to fill them in, than to get grilled while standing in front of twenty of your peers and managers.

My friend Don had to present a request for more funding for his Web site.

The management team looked over the request.

One challenged, "The growth projections for your Web site seem agressive. What makes you think you're going to get that many users?"

Don replied, "Well, according to Matrix Information and Directory Services, Web traffic has grown over fifty percent a month from early 1993 through the end of 1994. I don't see any sign of that slowing."

Don could answer any question thrown at him in a presentation or meeting. His secret? He would complete his work and then review it as if he were his own boss. He'd think, "Where might my boss ask for more information? Where's the hole in the argument? What follow-up questions will he ask based on this information?" Then he'd do the research to find the answers.

For his funding proposal, Don know he'd get asked why he thought the Web site would grow so quickly, so he got his data in advance.

The ultimate boss-question preparation happens for "Bill G Reviews." Throughout the year, project teams, from billion-dollar businesses to start-up ideas, present their progress to date, current status, and future plans to Bill Gates. Because Bill is known to probe everything from market-growth projections to the most intricate minutiae of emerging technologies, the teams go to inordinate lengths to know their stuff before they walk in the door. And while Bill does challenge and give direction, the true value of the meeting is often the depth and knowledge the team has gained from their prep work.

LESSON

MAKE DECISIONS AS IF YOU OWNED THE COMPANY

Whether you're deciding the direction of a new ad campaign or the timing of your new product launch, make your choice from a company perspective. Examine the ramifications your business decisions may have outside your area and ask yourself, "If I owned this company, what would I do? What would I want my employees to do?" Think beyond the scope of your responsibilities to the greater impact your actions may have.

There's a product called Microsoft Office that includes four kinds of business software in one box. Until a few years ago, you could only buy the pieces—a word processor, a spreadsheet, and so on—separately. When sales of this new combo pack started gaining momentum, the people working on the individual pieces had to decide on their advertising, direct mail, and other aspects of the marketing mix. And while they could have each gone their own way, with plans optimized to sell the most of their single product, they saw that a sale of all pieces together in Office benefited Microsoft more than a sale of their individual products. So even though they lost a great deal of their overall control and budget, they banded together to create one Office marketing message, Office ads, and Office direct mail.

For a time, the market share of the individual products suffered, but in the long run, Office's additional sales and users made up the shortfall. It's now best-selling software and has boosted its component products—Word, Excel, and PowerPoint—to the top spots in their categories.

Even big fish give way at Microsoft—to bigger fish. When multibillion-dollar-generator Office 95 went to market in the fall of 1995, it took a backseat to the marketing blitz of Windows 95 rather than compete with it. The Office team decided it would be better for Microsoft if Office rode the Windows 95 coattails rather than run separate, potentially competing, marketing activities. So they designed their boxes with blue and white clouds to look like Windows 95's, they appeared in the Windows 95 launch rather than have their own, and they touted their compatibility with Windows 95. The result was a unified message to customers about the Microsoft family of products. Office made its forecasted sales projection and spent less on its marketing than it would have had it gone out alone with a separate plan.

On a smaller scale, managers can face the same type of decision. In the consumer division, such popular CD-ROMs as Dinosaurs and Musical Instruments went to computer makers for unbelievably low prices so they would be bundled with new home computers. In this case, the product managers decided that customers' good experience with a high-quality Microsoft product would pave the way to increased sales of other Microsoft CD-ROMs. And that was more important than the profitability of a single product.

GETTING THE JOB DONE

LESSON

1   WORK SMART—NOT LONG

Unread memos, unending phone messages, overflowing to-do lists, a packed meeting schedule—you can get through anything if you organize and prioritize. Work smart instead of long. Cut unnecessary meetings. Don't be a perfectionist if it's not called for. Put your best efforts into the things that really matter to the business.

Rich Tong, vice president of the Windows NT business, comes in each morning and writes down three things he needs to do that day to make a difference to the company. If he gets more than three done, great, but this list has helped him prioritize at Microsoft for seven years, which he likens to "trying to drink from a fire hose."

Group Vice President Pete Higgins told a group of one hundred marketers, "Look at your objectives, your to-do list. It looks incredibly long. It **is** incredibly long. If you get priority one and two done, you'll do well." He tells his teams to go for the most bang for the buck, to rank high the responsibilities and assignments that impact the business most. Jon DeVaan, vice president in the Office software business, tells groups of programmers the same thing.

All of these senior managers know the value of cutting through the noise and getting to the heart of what is important to the business. They know that working smart can also mean taking pride in the things you **don't** do. A Microsoft product-development plan may list the features they're leaving out of the product and why. Managers may take pride in the meetings they don't go to or the memo distribution lists they get off of, showing that they're choosing only the key issues to focus on.

L E S S O N

2

"I DON'T KNOW" IS OKAY, ESPECIALLY COUPLED WITH "I'LL FIND OUT"

When a stumper comes up, those six little words "I don't know, I'll find out" are safer than bluffing. No one expects you to know everything, and a little humility can go a long way. "I don't know, I'll find out" shows you're honest, you're not panicking in the face of a challenge, and you're responsive, if you follow up with the answer.

A Microsoft product manager's nightmare goes something like this: You're in the company booth at a trade show, showing your product to a group of customers. You've got quite a crowd, including corporate customers and press people.

One person in the crowd says, "I have a question."

You tense up. You hope you can answer it.

The customer says, "I'm trying to create a RAM disk for my swapfile, but still have enough memory to run my real-mode TCP/IP stack. It's not working. What am I doing wrong?"

You have no idea. You barely understand half the vocabulary the customer used. And to add to your misery, your boss just happened to stop by at the back of the crowd.

"*Hmmmm*. It's hard to say without seeing your machine," you start to stammer. "Have you tried calling product support?"

"No, I was coming to the show today, so I thought I'd get it right from the product manager directly. You're in charge of the product aren't you?"

You gulp. The crowd smells blood and inches forward.

However, this is where you can end the nightmare and turn the situation around.

"I don't know the answer, so why don't I take your card and have someone call you when I get back to my office." The crowd looks skeptical.

"Here's my card, in case you want to contact me," you add, giving the customer assurance that you're not going to take his number and toss it the first chance you get. The crowd draws back. Out of the corner of your eye, you see your boss moving away to the next booth.

No one expects you to know everything. It's okay if you don't answer every obscure query that very second, as long as you promise to and do get an answer later.

Of course, if you don't want to get caught answerless, try to figure out in advance what the questions might be and the answers you'd give. Microsofties regularly go into trade shows, competitive contests, and press meetings prepared with a "rude Q&A" outlining the tough questions that might arise and the best answers.

The corollary to " 'I don't know' is okay" is, of course, "Don't make up an answer." In a meeting to plan a new product for home computers, a manager asked his market researcher a series of questions, including, "Are there any competitors in Germany and France yet?" The researcher paused, thinking there probably weren't, and then answered in a definite tone of voice, "No, there aren't." And so in the product plans, the team put off entering the big European markets, thinking they had time to do that later and still beat the competition. Two months later the team discovered that the competitors were indeed already in France and Germany. The researcher hadn't bothered to check the facts, guessing he pretty much knew them. He lost all credibility with the manager, even though the rest of his answers that day were correct. The manager no longer trusted his statements because he had represented a guess as a fact. The product also suffered in Europe, where it should have been given a higher priority and planned for with its competitors in mind.

LESSON

3

HUMOR CAN GET YOU OUT OF STICKY TIMES

We've all had embarrassing snafus, made foot-in-mouth comments, and had nightmare presentations where all the equipment stopped working. In most cases, a little self-deprecating humor can go a long way to ease the situation.

In one infamous incident at Microsoft, an employee was taken away in handcuffs by police—something to do with speeding and overdue tickets. Word of the incident got around quickly. Later the employee wanted to let people

▼ EASING TENSIONS, SPOOFING THE FIGHT ▲

The following joke E-mail message was sent around the Word development team after a spirited debate over naming different features.

TO:	Word Development Team
FROM:	Dean Hachamovitch
RE:	Suggestions for next version of Word

Word is so violent. Why does Microsoft call them bullets? They look like poppy seeds. Wouldn't the world be better if corporations didn't promote random violence with our terminology?

Why Paste Special? Shouldn't it really be ''Differently-capable Paste''?

Insert Object? Clearly designed by men.

''Normal'' view makes Page Layout and Outline feel inferior.

''Master Document'' view? Are other documents or views slaves? This reeks of colonialistic oppression.

Why are users encouraged to Insert Breaks? Shouldn't software work to heal the arbitrary divisions that have caused so much pain and suffering?

Tools menu? Whose tools are they?—clearly the oppressor's. For example, the only languages I found were Western European languages. Why won't they empower people outside the authoritarian regime?

know it was okay to mention it. He was in a meeting soon thereafter when police sirens were heard outside. "Excuse me, I've got to go," he said. "My ride is here." Soon, the news of the humorous remark had eclipsed the original incident.

Microsofties laugh at themselves with alarming regularity. Each year, the April 1 issue of the *Micronews* (Microsoft's employee newsletter) lampoons projects, policies, and company events. When Microsoft's new on-line magazine, *Slate,* was parodied on the Internet by a biting Web site called *Stale,* no one laughed harder than *Slate'*s publisher.

LESSON

4

REAL EMPLOYEES DO
EAT LUNCH

Microsoft managers know some of their employees might stay day and night working in their offices. And while that may sound like ideal worker behavior, they know a little break makes a lot of sense. And lots of important things happen outside the office.

Each of the cafeterias on the Microsoft main campus features a different menu. "This makes employees actually walk outside," says one manager. There are also volleyball courts, a jogging trail, and inexpensive health-club memberships, as well as Microsoft-sponsored nights at the symphony, museum, zoo, and theater, making it easy to enjoy Seattle's attractions. "You need to give your circuits a rest," one programmer points out. "I always come back refreshed after a cool concert or a great hike. Like my brain's been re-booted." (That's "restarted," for all you nondigerati.)

Staying in your office all day may be a great way to accomplish your tasks but may not make you the best at your job. In fact, you may be missing out on a host of information and opportunities by not hanging out with your colleagues. Some call this the dreaded "networking," but it's really just a way to find out what's happening around the company. Eight years ago, a group of young guys started having lunch together once a week. Some were in marketing; some were programmers. Over the years they traded stories, discussed technologies, moved around the company, got promoted. Throughout, they helped each other deal with thorny issues, gave each other the scoop on rising stars they noticed in their groups, and called each other to get things done when the usual systems were taking too long. They'd get together outside the office sometimes and once took a trip to Russia together. Now they're all vice presidents and directors in far-flung parts of Microsoft, and they still have their lunches, albeit less frequently. Their friendship, communication, and advice over the years has helped each succeed at Microsoft.

LESSON

5

CREATIVITY IS NOT A ONE-MAN JOB

Don't go it alone. When you're wrestling with a thorny issue or need a cool new idea, get your colleagues in on the action. You'll likely achieve greater results.

When designing Word for Windows, Dean Hachamovitch tried to figure out how to make Word's line-drawing capability easy enough for customers to use to make borders around paragraphs, tables, and pictures. After puzzling alone for days in his office, he went to one of his colleagues to see what he thought.

"Customers really want to make borders around their paragraphs," he explained, and drew some lines with a box around them on a piece of paper. "Or they want a shaded paragraph, or no border at all." He continued to draw. "Plus there are all these different kinds of lines they might want: thick, thin, dashed, doubled." He added the lines to his picture.

"Why don't you just show them that picture and they can click on the things they want?" his colleague asked.

Dean squinted. "Huh? Oh, yeah! Wow!"

All of a sudden Dean saw a solution that had been in front of him all along. It just took someone else to help him see it. The idea became part of the product. Layers of complicated commands disappeared. When users choose "Borders and Shading" from the Word menu, they are presented with the same simple visual choices that were drawn on a piece of paper that day.

When struggling with an idea—new marketing plans or a

competitive response—I'd sit in my office and think hard for a while. Write some stuff down. Go get a candy bar, and think some more. Then I'd usually call my team into my office for an informal brainstorming. I'd lay out the objective and the basic parameters, and we'd be off. Soon we'd all be yelling and tossing around thoughts. The room would fill up with ideas—some great, some useless—but the process brought out much more than it would have had I worked alone or if we each had worked on the same thing individually. I ended up with more high-quality ideas because the team members inspired one another. They felt valuable for having been called on to help, and if I ended up using their ideas, I gave them credit for it. This made them all the more eager to help next time.

I'd also go get advice from smart friends and old bosses in other areas of the company. Even just taking the time to logically lay out the question before I presented it sometimes provided an insight. And people mostly felt flattered rather than bothered when I asked "to borrow their brain."

LESSON

6

IF YOU'RE GOING TO DROP THE BALL, ARRANGE FOR SOMEONE TO CATCH IT

Sign up only for what you can really do. Whether it's signing up for a new project, an out-of-town business trip, or a follow-up call to a customer—if you can't do it, don't say you will. And if you can't follow through on a commitment, find help fast.

As you toil away at work, at some point you will likely realize you can't meet one of your commitments. We'll call it "X." First decide: "Is X important?" If X is **not** important, let your boss know that due to your other priorities you won't be able to do X, but you think it's okay for the business that it doesn't get done. If you think your boss may not know all the other stuff you're working on, list your other priorities for him or her! When you let your boss know, they have the option of

- reprioritizing your work so you can get X done and skip Y instead
- assigning X to another person
- agreeing X can be skipped (and now they know the reason why, in case it ever comes up in a meeting).

As an extra bonus, you save your butt in case your boss does think X is significant. One of the worst things a manager can hear is, "Oh, I never did that. I didn't think it was important."

Now, if you do think X **is** important, either

- examine your work priorities and find room for X by cutting Y, and let the boss know why you cut Y

- find someone else to do X, or to do Y so you can do X, and let the boss know who's taking over the new work

In either case, the message is the same, don't drop the ball without letting your boss know or getting someone to catch it for you. A few dropped balls and you'll find less important assignments coming your way or your boss hanging over you all the time, making sure you're doing your work. Save your sanity and the boss's by meeting your commitments.

LESSON

7

THEIR EXPERIENCE VS. YOUR INSTINCT

Sometimes you need to go with your gut, even when you disagree with the "experts."

As a Word product manager, I worked with the "Seminar team," who traveled the country showing Word, Excel, PowerPoint, and Project software to audiences of computer users. A large part of my responsibility was to review the seminar before it hit the road and make sure the team was talking about and showing Word in its best light.

We had a new version of Word going into the show. Research had shown that seminar attendees were interested more in the new products than the old, so I suggested the seminar invitation really highlight our new Word for Windows. I also asked that the seminar focus more time on Word, to show off its new features.

After a bit of discussion, the seminar director vetoed the idea and assured me that the right thing to do was to give all the products equal billing. When the next upgrades of Excel or PowerPoint were launched, she said, we'd still divide things up equally. I disagreed with this approach, but figured she was the expert on seminars.

As the seminars progressed, we realized people did indeed want to see more of the new product and less of the old. My manager asked me what had happened. I told him I didn't think it was right to evenly weight the products, but this wasn't my area of specialization. He shook his head and said, "Next time, if your instincts tell you something needs to change, fight harder. Trust yourself—you're smart. If you're unsure of how to press and how hard, come to me. Don't be afraid to escalate." That summer, I got my first less-than-stellar raise when review time came around—I also worked on discovering my backbone.

LESSON

8

WORK FAUX PAS

It's easy to make social and professional gaffes on the job. Here are some I've seen at Microsoft that you may want to avoid.

- Don't print out your performance review on a communal printer, and then leave it out overnight. The same goes for job listings you're secretly pursuing.
- If you want to keep your office romance secret, don't call your boss early in the morning from your boyfriend's (or girlfriend's) home phone—Murphy's Law says your boss will have caller ID.
- Don't ridicule inept summer interns—they may be related to a top executive.
- Don't write sarcastic things in drafts of serious memos, expecting that you'll take them out before sending the final version. You'll inevitably forget.
- Don't be a competitive jerk on the office softball team. Everyone will remember it at work the next day.

▼   **GETTING THE JOB DONE, THE REAL MICROSOFT WAY?**   ▲

From an email message forwarded around the company
spoofing Microsoft's work hard culture

TO:	Team
FROM:	?
RE:	BURNOUT PREVENTION AND RECOVERY: Health Tips for the 90s and Their Microsoft Counterparts

1
STOP DENYING

Listen to the wisdom of your body. Begin to freely admit
the stresses and pressures which have manifested
physically, mentally, or emotionally.

MICROSOFT VIEW: Work until the physical pain forces you
into unconsciousness.

2
AVOID ISOLATION

Don't do everything alone! Develop or renew intimacies
with friends and loved ones. Closeness not only brings new
insights, but also is anathema to agitation and depression.

MICROSOFT VIEW: Shut your office door and lock it from
the inside so no one will distract you. They're just trying to
hurt your productivity.

3
CHANGE YOUR CIRCUMSTANCES

If your job, your relationships, a situation, or a person is
dragging you under, try to alter your circumstances or, if
necessary, leave.

MICROSOFT VIEW: If you feel something is dragging you
down, suppress these thoughts. This is a weakness. Drink
more coffee. (It's free.)

4
DIMINISH INTENSITY IN YOUR LIFE

Pinpoint those areas or aspects which summon up the
most concentrated intensity and work toward alleviating
that pressure.

MICROSOFT VIEW: Increase intensity. Maximum intensity = maximum productivity. If you find yourself relaxed and with your mind wandering, you are probably having a detrimental effect on the stock price.

5
STOP OVERNURTURING

If you routinely take on other people's problems and responsibilities, learn to gracefully disengage. Try to get some nurturing for yourself.

MICROSOFT VIEW: Always attempt to do everything. You ARE responsible for it all. Perhaps you haven't thoroughly read your job description.

6
LEARN TO SAY "NO"

You'll help diminish intensity by speaking up for yourself. This means refusing additional requests or demands on your time or emotions.

MICROSOFT VIEW: Never say no to anything. It shows weakness and lowers the stock price. Never put off until tomorrow what you can do at midnight.

7
BEGIN TO BACK OFF AND DETACH

Learn to delegate, not only at work, but also at home and with friends. In this case, detachment means rescuing yourself for yourself.

MICROSOFT VIEW: Delegating is a sign of weakness. Let someone else do it (see #5).

8
REASSESS YOUR VALUES

Try to sort out the meaningful values from the temporary and fleeting, the essential from the nonessential. You'll conserve energy and time, and begin to feel more centered.

MICROSOFT VIEW: Stop thinking about your own problems. This is selfish. If your values change, we will make an announcement at the company meeting. Until then, if someone calls you and questions your priorities, tell them that you are unable to comment on this and give them the number for Microsoft Marketing. It will be taken care of.

9
LEARN TO PACE YOURSELF

Try to take life in moderation. You only have so much energy available. Ascertain what is wanted and needed in your life, then begin to balance work with love, pleasure, and relaxation.

MICROSOFT VIEW: A balanced life is a myth perpetuated by the Lotus Marketing Team. Don't be a fool: the only thing that matters is work and productivity.

10
TAKE CARE OF YOUR BODY

Don't skip meals, abuse yourself with rigid diets, disregard your need for sleep, or break doctor appointments. Take care of yourself nutritionally.

MICROSOFT VIEW: Your body serves your mind, your mind serves the company. Push the mind and the body will follow. Drink Mountain Dew. (It's free.)

11
DIMINISH WORRY AND ANXIETY

Try to keep superstitious worrying to a minimum—it changes nothing. You'll have a better grip on your situation if you spend less time worrying and more time taking care of your real needs.

MICROSOFT VIEW: If you're not worrying about work, you must not be very committed to it. We'll find someone who is.

12
KEEP YOUR SENSE OF HUMOR

Begin to bring joy and happy moments into your life. Very few people suffer burnout when they're having fun.

MICROSOFT VIEW: So, you think your work is funny? We'll discuss this with your manager on Friday. At 7:00 pm.

MANAGING YOUR MANAGER

L E S S O N

1

MAKE YOUR BOSS
LOOK GOOD

The perfect symbiotic relationship at work: you try to make your boss a star and the boss does the same for you.

Once our team got T-shirts that said "Jon [our boss] is great" on the front and "My job is to make Jon look great" on the back. The T-shirts were meant as a joke, but it's basically true that your job is to make your boss look great. When your manager looks good, you look good. You are associated with a winner, and upper management views your team as the one to turn to with new challenges and opportunities.

Keep your boss informed, give him or her honest feedback, and support his or her decisions with your best efforts. You will make your boss shine, and the boss is likely to respond by giving you strong reviews and proper credit with upper management and letting you take on more challenging assignments. You'll both look great as part of a well-oiled team.

LESSON

2

DON'T WASTE YOUR BOSS'S TIME

Be aware of your boss's time. Does the boss want to be included in all meetings, on all memos, and E-mail, or does he or she prefer summaries from you? Does your boss encourage you to "stop by anytime," or should you save unscheduled visits for the most urgent issues?

One of my team members would ask for five minutes of my time, but then stay in my office for an hour. Another would ramble through the background of a situation rather than cutting straight to the problem, question, or outcome. Both wasted valuable time by not thinking through what the meeting really should cover.

If you need a longish meeting, schedule it in advance. And don't use your boss's time to think a problem through for the first time if you could have done that on your own beforehand.

LESSON

3

BRING SOLUTIONS, NOT PROBLEMS

When you come to your boss with a question or problem, bring along a few possible solutions.

Early in my time at Microsoft, I went through a period when I thought everything was a disaster. People wouldn't listen to me, so I'd "have" to go to my boss, Jon, and bring him in as the heavy.

After a few of these fire drills, he said, "Bring me solutions, not problems. Don't come and tell me the direct-mail team won't use your idea. Tell me the direct-mail team won't use your idea so you've thought of three other ideas that take their concerns into account. Tell me why you discarded ideas one and two and why you recommend number three. Once you've taken a good first pass at it, I can help advise you."

I tried it out and it worked. In most situations, by the time I had really thought the problem through, I had come up with solutions I could implement myself. I didn't have to bother Jon at all. And in those cases where I did go to him, I presented my options and the logic I had used to analyze them. As long as I did my up-front analysis and thought through the situation, Jon was happy to help me examine the possibilities. He listened and recommended—a far better use of his time. When I became a manager, I passed on his advice, "Bring me solutions, not problems."

4

PREPARE YOUR MANAGER FOR BAD NEWS EARLY

Don't surprise your boss with a missed deadline, public relations nightmare, or production glitch. If trouble is brewing, let the boss know as soon as possible. Your personal "early warning system" gives your manager time to either help you, defend you, or prepare you or upper management for what's to come.

One of the high-profile CD-ROM teams worked hard all summer to get their new product into stores for the big Christmas selling season. The going was tough, but they remained optimistic about meeting their deadlines. They even put out press releases to get everyone ready for big Christmas sales. Now, optimism is fine, but they neglected to discuss with their manager the risks they were facing and the small delays that were happening along the way.

As time went on, the programmers had to work harder just to make up missed goals. Every stage seemed to take longer and expose more problems than they had expected. Still, they failed to tell their boss the accurate status of the schedule and the product. Their weekly progress reports showed little sign of the impending doom. "Optimism overcame reality," their manager told me later.

Finally, late in the fall, they saw that their attempts were futile. They were going to miss the Christmas sales season. They broke the bad news to their manager, taking him totally by surprise. This was also an especially bad time to tell their boss. He was going in for a project review with Bill Gates that week to cover the status of the CD-ROMs coming for Christmas.

When the manager told Bill his team's CD-ROM was not going to make Christmas, Bill angrily wanted to know why they had discovered this so late, after the press releases and other marketing activities had begun. The manager tried to explain the complexities of the product. Bill cut him off. The manager tried to explain the dependence on a new technology they were using. Bill cut him off. The manager stopped trying to explain as Bill peppered him about how much money this would cost, what kind of black eye we'd get with software stores for overpromising, why, as a manager, you had to know these things in advance, and on and on. The meeting basically turned into the manager's worst nightmare.

If, instead of waiting until the last minute, the programmers had come in at the early stages saying, "It looks like we may have a problem. This is why. Here are some possible alternatives," their manager might have been able to help solve the problem, might have halted related activities (the marketing spending, in this case), and if he couldn't solve the problem, he could have let his managers know earlier, avoiding the confrontation with Bill.

LESSON

5

SEE HOW YOUR BOSS WORKS AND WHAT (S)HE NEEDS

Always figure out how your managers like to work. What are their strengths and how can you learn from them? What are their weaknesses and how can you help shore them up? Don't be afraid to ask them how they prefer to work, or confirm with them what you've noticed so far.

Aid your boss where he or she needs it most. One friend of mine saw that her new boss hated crunching numbers. So she volunteered to prepare the monthly sales-data report. Another Microsoftie noticed he was much more creative than his manager, so he switched on overdrive his idea generation at brainstorming sessions. A good manager knows his or her weaknesses and may have hired you for your complementary strength. Use it.

LESSON

6

LET 'EM KNOW HOW
THEY'RE DOING

*If you don't let your boss know how he or she is doing,
how can you expect your boss to change?*

My boss Paul had some bad habits. In team meetings he'd respond to ideas half-jokingly/half-rudely, "That will be duly noted and ignored" or "Why don't we move on." Sometimes he'd just make a loud noise like a wrong-answer buzzer in a game show. Meeting one-on-one, he'd stand over your desk, pointing a Nerf weapon at you. His favorite activity was drawing the organization chart and pointing out that you were at the bottom of it.

Sometimes managers need feedback. Paul did, so we gave it to him. Some things we mentioned in a joking way. On the Nerf issue, I said in a parental voice, "We're going to have to take those toys away if you can't use them responsibly. Now, stop pointing them at people." In other areas, the more senior people spoke up for the junior ones: "I think you intimidate Jack and Cynthia in meetings. Have you noticed they don't speak up that much anymore? Maybe you shouldn't be so harsh."

On other topics, we just let him know, in a straightforward way, what he did that we didn't like and why. We also told him the good things he did so he wouldn't think that all his habits were bad. He listened and cleaned up his act. He still keeps a Nerf rifle in his office, but he's now regarded as one of the best managers in the company by the people who have worked for him.

Does your manager's closed-door policy and insistence on

relying on E-mail strangle communication? Does your boss change his or her mind on decisions you thought were all set? Say something to your boss. Do it in a positive, constructive way. If you don't do anything to let them know, they won't have a clue that they're not doing everything perfectly. Bosses, like most of us, do not read minds.

Great managers are made, not born. Sometimes they are made by their teams.

LESSON

7

GIVE YOUR BOSS
TWO CHANCES

If your boss is screwing up, discuss the problem with him or her directly rather than going over your boss's head to his or her boss. If your boss doesn't improve, warn your boss before you do go over his or her head.

My colleague Lori came to me complaining about her boss. "Sandy is smart and all, but I never see her. She blows off our weekly meetings. She's never in her office, and when I do see her, it's for five minutes before I'm rushed out. She also changes her mind after she's given me the go-ahead on things. I want to switch jobs!"

"Have you talked to Sandy about this?" I asked.

"Well, no," she replied.

"Why don't you lay out your concerns to her and suggest a specific solution, such as sticking with your weekly meetings but making them shorter? And ask her how she prefers you to communicate to her the decision deadlines she needs to meet—E-mail, Post-It notes on her PC, whatever."

Lori agreed to open the communication lines with Sandy, and she let her know her concerns. Sandy agreed the areas needed improvement and said she'd change. But she did not change.

Lori went back to her one more time saying, "Last time we spoke, you said you'd make it to all your meetings with me and review things by the date I needed your input. Of our last six meetings, you've missed three, and you've changed your mind twice on projects I thought were done. If we can't work this out, I need to go talk to Robbie (Sandy's boss) to figure out what to do because this is really impeding my job performance."

This both motivated and warned Sandy. She didn't want her employee complaining to her boss, so she did indeed change! The majority of managers take constructive suggestions quite well, but some seem to need a little more prodding than others. And they don't want their team complaining up one level.

LESSON

8

IF YOU BAIL OUT FROM A BAD BOSS

"Your manager can either be a speedboat for your career or an anchor on it," says one Microsoftie. If you're stuck with an anchor and you can't stand it anymore, plan your escape. Try to leave on the best terms possible. If you can, let your boss know in advance that you are looking to make a move, rather than springing a transfer on your boss that may leave him or her in the lurch. If possible, supply your boss with a replacement for the spot you're leaving.

My friend Steve just plain had a bad boss. He'd take Steve's reports, put his own name at the top, and send them around. He would agree with Steve on an idea but not back him up if that idea got shot down in a meeting by someone higher up in the food chain. He sent Steve on a grueling five-day customer-visit trip that covered Texas, Chicago, New York, and Ohio, while he attended the Microsoft national sales meeting in Hawaii.

Steve tried to make the best of his situation but to no avail. So he planned to make as easy an exit as possible. Steve worked as hard as he could on his projects, continued writing the reports his manager put his name to, and never bad-mouthed his manager (this is key because it *will* get back to them). He also looked for other opportunities. He let his manager know he needed a change, mentioning some career criteria that his current job couldn't offer. And finally, to make his manager more comfortable with his move, he helped find a replacement and agreed to stay through the new employee's first week to train him.

LESSON

9

DON'T BURN BRIDGES

Always do your best for your boss and colleagues. You never know when they'll turn up again.

Sometimes corporate folks are asked to fly out to a local sales office to help close a big deal. One young marketer agreed to make a trip to a Midwest sales office and then canceled four times before the sales manager finally told him to forget it. Unhappily for the marketer, the sales manager took a job at headquarters—as the marketer's new boss. He greeted the young marketer with the words, "Beware! The toes you stepped on yesterday are connected to the derriere you must kiss today!"

Old bosses can turn up anywhere. You may work for them again. Or you may need them for favors, recommendations, quick information, or advice, so leave them on the best possible terms with the best possible impression. As a ten-week summer intern, I worked hard and tried to please my boss. By the time I came back to work full-time, things in the group had changed and my boss was in another division. Six years and two Microsoft jobs later, a reorganization landed me back in her office. Melinda French, general manager of a major CD-ROM group, was my boss again and now Bill Gates's wife!

3 ALL I REALLY NEED TO KNOW TO BE A GOOD BOSS I LEARNED AT MICROSOFT

Just because you're the leader, doesn't mean your team knows when, how, why, and where to follow. You need to guide your employees. Sound simple? Then why are there so many I-can't-believe-my-boss-did-that stories? Feedback, goals, and deadlines will keep your team on track. Giving credit for good work isn't just great for morale; it will benefit you as well. Strong employees always have their pick of opportunities, and stars gravitate toward strong managers. And really, you want all of your employees to shine—after all, they reflect on you.

LEADING

L E S S O N

1

COMMUNICATE THE STRATEGY

You want your team to make the right decision. And ideally you want them to make it without having to ask you. Communicate the overall strategy or goals, and let your team take it from there.

Chris Peters, a Microsoft vice president, is a quirky programmer who makes his own Tabasco sauce and created an Internet Web site called the Bureau of Atomic Tourism. His favorite food is Peeps, neon yellow Easter marshmallow chicks, and he is one of the best managers at Microsoft. Chris is known for setting out simple, clear priorities. When creating Word 6.0 for Windows, Chris announced three product goals to his team.

He told them Word 6.0 had to be

1. "auto-everything" (make everyday tasks, such as spell-checking and formatting, automatic)
2. a great part of the Office suite (consistent look and good interaction with Microsoft's spreadsheet and graphics software)
3. the best upgrade for WordPerfect users (high-quality help and file filters)

Simply put, these goals drove the success of Microsoft's billion-dollar word-processing business. The goals were easy to understand. Word processors had gotten overly complex, jammed full of features that few people used. "Auto-every-thing" got back to basics. Only this time, instead of just helping you get your work done, the computer would actually do it for you, by automatically numbering lists, correcting spelling, and so on. Goal number two stemmed from observing the market. With more people using software applications together and Lotus's Smart Suite office-software collection gaining ground, it made sense to focus next on making our office software act alike and work alike. And finally, the largest untapped (for us) word-processing segment, WordPerfect users, had started defecting to Word. Capture more of these users, and Word's growth would far outpace the rest of the market's.

Armed with this straightforward set of directions, the team went to work. Every person on the team, and there were over two hundred, could spout the three priorities if you stopped them in the hallway. If a new feature did not match up to one of those three priorities, it was not included in the new version. There were hundreds of features that could have been added to this version of Word, but every programmer, tester, and planner knew if a feature didn't match up to the one of the three goals—to cut it.

The programmers made trade-offs and moved forward based on Chris's guidelines. They didn't need to go to him for decisions because they understood his priorities.

The simplicity and clarity of Chris's priorities provided an additional boon. It made the new benefits easy to communicate to customers. So in turn, the marketing team and sales force created product demonstrations, data sheets, direct-mail pieces, ads, corporate seminars, and other marketing materials based on the three goals of the product. A year later, the product was completed and Word 6.0 entered the market. For the first time in its ten-year history, it became the world's best-selling word processor, overtaking rival WordPerfect.

LESSON

2   GIVE YOUR TEAM TIME

One short meeting a week with each team member can keep them from spinning their wheels in the wrong direction for the next forty hours (or eighty, in some places!). Your quick response on a plan submitted for your review keeps the team moving, rather than waiting. Give your time when your group needs it and your time will go a long way.

Microsoft managers have devised lots of ways to make themselves available to their teams and still get their own work done. Director of Consumer Division Marketing Ruthann Lorentzen, a frenetic, sharp, and pithy marketer, had an unusual open-door policy. You could stop by at any time of the day or night when she was in. But you only had two minutes to state your case, hear her answer, and get out. Ruthann's laserlike intensity was disconcerting to some, but it taught us to be prepared with clear, concise reports and information, and we knew she was always accessible. Another manager, who hated interruptions, put up office hours like a college professor to let his team know the best time to stop by.

It's easy to overlook people's questions and requests during a busy day, especially if you don't know how urgent their issue is or the deadline they're facing. One product planner asked his team to note on the top of any memo or header of any E-mail they submitted the date by which they needed his response.

On-going availability is important, but so are scheduled

periodic check-ins. Microsofties call these weekly meetings "one-on-ones." They may be fifteen minutes long, one hour, or just covered by a summary E-mail, but people see one-on-ones as a chance to check in, talk about progress or problems, get feedback, or reprioritize their work. These meetings keep the managers abreast of their teams' work and ensure that the teams aren't going off on a decision path or assignment that doesn't make sense. Most of my managers also used one-on-ones to check on my six-month objectives (every Microsoftie has a set) and see if I was delivering on the bigger picture.

LESSON

3

GIVE YOUR TEAM A HILL TO CLIMB

Whether you're banded together to meet a deadline, to fight a competitor, or just to beat the team down the hall, a challenging rival can be a great motivator. And a little competition can make a big difference.

From the mid eighties, Word's big competitor was always WordPerfect. So the Word for Windows team studied WordPerfect's market share, units sold, the programs they ran, and who their big corporate customers were. WordPerfect ads appeared in the hallway tacked up alongside Word's ads. One programmer put up a sign that read, "It's about WordPerfect, Stupid," harkening back to Clinton's '92 campaign. Another had a picture of WordPerfect's CEO taped to her monitor so it stared at her all day long. We were in second place and intent on moving to the number one spot. We were focused. We were motivated. We forged ahead.

When we finally pulled in front of WordPerfect, our own sister product Microsoft Excel (the spreadsheet) became our competitor. Chris Peters, then head of the Word business, now a vice president, would ask, "What are our COGs?" ("*cost of goods sold*"—the price to put a box of Word together in the factory).

We told him.

"Is it a dollar less than Excel's?" he demanded.

It wasn't.

"Let's get our costs below Excel's. Tell me next week how we're going to do it."

We trundled off to examine our box of Word and figure out if we could remove, combine, or reduce anything. We met with the manufacturing team and ended up squeezing a little out of the cost, saving the company hundreds of thousands of dollars over the next few months and, best of all, beating Excel.

Chris exhorted us to do better than the team next-door, and we took up the challenge. The friendly rivalry spilled over into volleyball matches and funny poems, but we'd really concentrate on things like creating the best sales-force aids, customer profiles, and international-subsidiary training kits that we could so we could get the ultimate satisfaction—the Excel team's managers telling them to "Do it like Word did." The Excel team tried to do the same. We were focused. We were motivated. Both teams forged ahead.

4

GIVE CREDIT

"Great job!" can go a long way. And it's cheaper and easier to push through than a raise or promotion. Giving credit boosts morale and makes your team work harder for you because they know they'll be recognized for it.

The first time a friend of mine received a congratulatory E-mail from Bill Gates, he printed it out, told his mom, and had it framed. If you haven't warranted the attention of the CEO, there's still recognition to be had at Microsoft. Teams give out a variety of awards at meetings. Jon Reingold, Excel's general manager, presents "Rheiny" awards at his business-unit meetings—small plastic rhinos for a job well done. When Vice President Brad Chase headed up Windows marketing, he gave "Wild Goose" (chase) awards. As head of the Kids software group, Charlotte Guyman gave out "Charlatte" awards—certificates for a free latte from the cafeteria to employees who had gone above and beyond. These awards may take little time or budget but can help inspire the team and build a sense of loyalty.

One manager totaled up his product's sales, estimated his team's weight, and announced in a meeting, "I always knew you were a great team, but today you are officially worth your weight in gold." Sales continued their uptick, and a few months later he proclaimed they were now worth their weight in platinum.

Microsoft has had its share of flops, though, in the employee-recognition area. One year, thousands of employees who had worked to build products received identical plaques that were inscribed, "To honor your individual achievement." Many plaques ended up as doorstops.

Reward the values you want to perpetuate. At Microsoft, formal and informal awards go to folks for writing great computer code, selling the most software, innovating new product features, or finding a better solution to an old problem—not for working the most hours. These awards are sparse and meaningful, not devalued by appearing in large numbers.

LESSON

5   AND TAKE BLAME

The flip side of giving credit for good things is taking the onus for bad ones. Don't blame another team member, your own group, or another organization for a problem, whatever it is. If you're the manager and ultimately responsible, you'll gain the respect of higher-ups and the loyalty of your team if you take on the burden, no matter whose fault the problem was.

When it became obvious in a meeting with Bill Gates that the Microsoft sales force had been ill equipped over the previous six months to sell a new E-mail product, Jeff Raikes, the head of the sales force, didn't rant and rave about how the E-mail product team had failed to give his people the information and selling tools they needed. He didn't blame his own staff for not flagging the problem early on. He didn't fault the front-line sales managers for not finding solutions when their salespeople started bringing the problem to their attention.

While some or all of the above may have been at fault, Jeff simply said, "We were ill prepared for the launch, and it cost us in sales. Next time we will take the following steps to make sure we are totally ready . . ." and proceeded to talk about some of the problems and how they'd be fixed. He looked good for taking the blame and handling the problem calmly. His staff and the E-mail product team were relieved not to get skewered. They knew they had gotten off easy and made a mental note to fix things next time. And the salespeople saw that Jeff was personally going to make sure the problem wouldn't happen again.

LESSON

6

ACT THE WAY YOU WANT
YOUR TEAM TO ACT

Your behavior as a leader has a direct effect on your group. They take cues from your attitudes and actions. As your group becomes larger or you become more senior, your example can even be a significant factor in setting the corporate culture.

Bill Gates almost always flies coach. Executive Vice President Steve Ballmer carries his own computer equipment and bags on press tours. He'll also stay up until 2 AM with a team working on a presentation to get the job done. Steve didn't even own a suit in 1991, although he was worth over one billion dollars. Showy is not Microsoft style. Hard work and conservative spending is.

You'll see these attitudes throughout the company. Programmers in the Office software group think nothing of staying until midnight for "workaholic Wednesdays," the night that weekly goals are due. Seminar presenters finish one session in one city, fly to the next, and make sure all the equipment and demos are set up before they fall into bed. The attire throughout Microsoft also reflects the low-key executives. Project T-shirts touting Windows NT, the Comdex trade show, or a new CD-ROM far outnumber expensive watches or ironed shirts.

Even mannerisms and sayings are passed down. Whether it's rocking back and forth in a chair like Bill Gates concentrating in a meeting or using buzzwords like "bandwidth," "leverage," or "demo hell," the corporate culture is apparent.

LESSON

7

SEND YOUR TEAM IN TO BILL GATES

When a big meeting or presentation comes along, try giving the assignment to someone who works for you. Putting a team member in front of the head honcho shows that you trust this person to know his or her stuff and do a good job. Coach the individual along the way and give him or her the opportunity to shine.

A "Bill" meeting, where a team presents a plan or product to Bill Gates, is a sometimes exhilarating, always terrifying, rite of passage. At these notoriously tough sessions, present-ers are grilled, challenged, yelled at, and every so often con-gratulated. "Bill stories" find their way into Microsoft lore. In one favorite, often told to first-time presenters, Bill is said to have shouted at a young marketer, "Do we pay you?! Do we actually pay you?!"

When I was a product manager in the Consumer Divi-sion, three people worked for me, and each was responsible for a product area. In our first month, we found out that each set of products was scheduled to present to Bill in three weeks. Usually, the most senior people on the teams attend the "Bill" meetings. In this case, though, I sent one member of my team to each meeting to represent us. After the initial terror wore off, they were glad for the opportunity.

The team sweated and prepared for the big day. They did a practice run-through, peppering each other with questions. "Scared but Prepared" was their motto as they marched into what seemed like the lion's den. They brought piles of data to flip through, just in case.

One new product idea, a gardening CD-ROM, was presented.

"What makes you think this will sell?" Bill asked.

The young product manager, heart palpitating, reeled off three sources of data showing what a popular hobby gardening was, the dollars spent on gardening each year, and how it overlapped with our target market of home PC owners.

Bill nodded and moved on to technical questions.

The marketer breathed an audible sigh of relief, which caused a few to chuckle. He wasn't called on again. He emerged unscathed and victorious.

L E S S O N

8

PREPARE A CLASS OF SUCCESSES, NOT A SUCCESSOR

The best way to get out of your job and move on is to train someone on your team to take over. Your boss will feel comfortable letting you go, your employee will be motivated to work hard to get your job, and you will be free! But better yet, grow the whole team rather than one heir. One may still rise to the top, but the whole group and the company will be better off if they're all ready for the next level.

As manager of Excel marketing, Hank Vigil worked on building a successful organization. By challenging his entire team with tougher and tougher assignments, and debating important issues and decisions with them, he made sure they were all trained to take on the next promotion. He encouraged them to think creatively and to try new things.

Each member of the group broke new ground. They started Microsoft's first direct-mail program, first seminars, first try-before-you-buy versions of the products. They established new research metrics and broadened their public relations successes from the industry to the general press. Hank made sure his whole team had the skills to meet current and upcoming business needs. So, rather than producing one successor, the whole team spun off successfully to be leaders of other areas. Five years later, Hank's old team, now scattered around the company, are all high-level managers.

GETTING THROUGH ROUGH SPOTS

L E S S O N

---

1   IT'S ALMOST NEVER AS BAD AS YOU THINK IT IS

No matter what your team, partner, or agency has done, losing your temper almost never helps the situation. Letting people calmly own up to and fix mistakes repairs the damage efficiently with the fewest ulcers and helps you plan for the next time.

When Ron Souza worked in the Consumer Division, he always remained calm. Once, a direct-mail piece went to two hundred thousand customers with the phone number of a local Seattle pet shop on it instead of our customer service line. Another time, one thousand sales people were told about a product that was supposed to be completely and totally under wraps. He just asked his three magic questions:

- How did this happen?
- What can we do to fix it?
- What can we do so it doesn't happen again?

We all remained calm because he remained calm and went about fixing the problem. We weren't afraid to admit our mistakes because Ron always remained unruffled. No possibility of severe punishments or wild tirades loomed over our heads. If he had yelled and created a lot of noise over a mistake, we would have been focused less on the problem and more on his anger. Buoyed by Ron's composure, we just focused on trying to repair the damage and making sure the situation wouldn't be repeated.

2

STAY FLEXIBLE—YOUR JOB MAY CHANGE COMPLETELY IN SIX MONTHS

It's great to "plan your work and work your plan," but it's just as important to know when to scrap the plan entirely and work like crazy on something new.

Every six months each Microsoft employee commits to a set of objectives, which have been agreed to by his or her manager. As a result of writing their objectives themselves, the employees become masters of their own destinies, signing up for only what they can handle. Microsoft uses "S.M.A.R.T." objectives:

- Specific
- Measurable/Observable
- Accountable/Attainable
- Results-based
- Timebound

The objectives may change along the way, but starting off with SMART objectives gives people direction and priorities. As a Microsoft manager, I pulled out my team's lists of objectives every month or so to review them with each individual, noting which items were completed, what was done well, where there were glitches, and what still needed to get done. This helped avoid performance-review surprises and big deviations from the goals we had both agreed to.

That said, sometimes radical things happen that entirely change your objectives or your group's objectives. The flip side of following your plan is knowing when to scrap it and form another. As the marketing manager in charge of Word, Excel, and PowerPoint in December of 1995, Michael Hebert did not even once use the word "Internet" as he wrote his six-month objectives. On January 15 he was informed that Microsoft planned to buy a company called Vermeer that produced software that allowed people to create their own Web pages on the Internet.

One week later, Michael and his team had put together a press release, customer information for the sales force, information for Microsoft's Internet site, and informed Microsoft's international subsidiaries of the new company, product, and plans. That winter and spring, his team helped launch two new products from the new company and interviewed and hired folks to do the marketing. By June, the group's performance reviews bore little resemblance to their original objectives.

LESSON

3

BE THE DESIGNATED JERK FOR YOUR TEAM

"Good cop—bad cop" can work in the business world.

The marketing team came to a meeting to hear the plans made by the sales team for their holiday products. The sales team proceeded to lay out ideas that in no way, shape, or form met the marketers expectations. But the marketers stayed quiet and calm. They knew their boss, "the tornado," would come in and argue, yell, cajole, threaten, and finally sweet-talk the sales team into providing what his marketing group needed.

Their boss called himself the Designated Jerk because his role as the bad guy left his team's working relationship with the sales group intact. The sales group might resent the marketers' boss, but they saw the marketing team as the good guys, the folks who worked hard with them day to day.

The boss made sure to let his team know he was being a jerk just temporarily for the meeting so they wouldn't emulate him! At other times he was the Designated Scapegoat or Designated Peacemaker.

LESSON

4

BENEATH YOU? NOT
BENEATH THE RESULTS

As you gain experience, become a manager, and generally rise through the ranks, you may be called on to do "scut work." Do it. It's something the business needs, you'll look like a team player, and people will do you favors in the future.

Lots of Microsoft managers roll up their sleeves and help the team through a crunch. Head programmers stay late with their teams on "workaholic Wednesdays," checking on new computer code. Marketing managers sit in hallways putting together holiday mailers if the deadline is near and the need arises. Once manager personally took the ten pieces that would make up a new software box and brought them to a post office to get weighed because the manufacturing plant needed mailing costs to estimate their shipping. Executive Vice President Mike Maples made and served his own grits at an employee thank-you breakfast. "It's crazy but these things really count," a breakfast eater commented between bites.

So do what it takes to get the job done. It makes sense for you and the business.

A GOOD BOSS GETS THE BEST TEAM

LESSON

1

MANAGE YOUR TEAM ONE PERSON AT A TIME

Sometimes your team is a team. More often they are a group of individuals, and each needs to be managed differently.

The people on one team I managed might as well have been from different planets. They ran the gamut of skills and commitment:

THE NEW GUY

Jared, my most junior team member, had just joined Microsoft. As a typical new employee, he was super-excited to be there but not exactly sure what to do. He had tons of commitment but few skills. He needed more than the usual amount of guidance, feedback, and praise, since he didn't know much about his job or the company culture yet.

I checked in with him often. I made sure his six-month objectives were superdetailed. To help get him settled, and to reduce the time I needed to spend with him, I assigned him an informal mentor whom he could go to and ask "stupid questions." His mentor treated this as a manager-in-training assignment.

Jared got going in fits and starts. He brought a can of Coke into a meeting with Pepsi corporate customers. He asked a high-level manager (a woman in her forties) to make him some copies, thinking she was an administrative assistant. It took him a while, but he eventually got the hang of things and is now a fully functional and valuable team member.

THE UNDERPERFORMER

My next team member, David, had been at the job awhile, knew what he was doing, but his enthusiasm seesawed. He was skilled but not committed, doing great work on the assignments he liked and practically ignoring the rest. He needed less direction and more support.

I tried to get him one hundred percent committed as a team member by making sure he had the resources to get his job done, recognizing his efforts, and matching his intersts to his responsibilities when possible. My favorite trick was to assign him part of a team project, since I knew he wouldn't want to embarrass himself by letting down his peers. I also gave him lots of public praise when he did high quality work so he'd be motivated to do more of the same. His performance improved, but it took constant time and effort to get him there and keep him there.

THE STAR

My star, Jennifer, needed little guidance, time, or detailed instruction. She was both skilled and committed. Some feedback was still important to make course corrections and give encouragement, but she pretty much did her own thing. Two pitfalls I had to watch out for here: I had to make sure my star was constantly challenged and recognized so she wouldn't get bored and look for other opportunities in another position, and I also made sure not to get lulled into the idea that she was doing so well that I never needed to see her or check in with her. Too little attention can set your star adrift and make them feel abandoned.

Talk about your stars with other managers—let the word get out about them. When it looks as if they're outgrowing their job, help them find the best opportunity possible. It's painful to lose them, but good for the company and the employees to keep them challenged and learning. You'll get kudos for fostering their rise, and there's nothing like the loyalty of a colleague you've helped.

THE PROCRASTINATOR

My last team member, Karl, a recent college grad, pulled ''all-nighters'' before any big assignment was due. This habit was a university leftover and had worked well for him for the previous four years. Unfortunately for Karl, Microsoft projects often involve getting some help or data from others (who weren't around at 4 AM), so his work was often shoddy, poorly organized, and incomplete.

I took a lesson from Pete Higgins, a group vice president, who often asks for milestones—check-in points along the way—from any team or person working on a big project, whether it's developing a piece of software or writing a memo.

For my college grad's next big assignment, I asked for a time line. When would he collect his data? When would he have his preliminary findings? When would he have a written outline of his report? When would the draft and final report be completed? I told him that at each milestone I'd like to meet with him briefly to hear his preliminary findings, see his outline, and so on. He looked aghast, but this forced him to plan out his work in smaller chunks and meet more deadlines along the way.

This time, he did quality work on time. I had to spend an inordinate amount of energy shepherding him toward getting the assignment done, but as he got used to his newly imposed work style, he needed less and less guidance.

2

MENTOR YOUR TEAM

Grow your employees, They benefit, you benefit, and the company benefits. Whether it's a challenging new assignment or lunch with you and your colleagues, make ways to help your team get to the next level of performance and responsibility.

One day my boss walked into my office saying, "Pete wants to know if we should have toll-free customer support for Word. WordPerfect's got it, and they're always touting it. Can you take a week to figure out if we should have it and then give him your recommendations?"

Pete was our division vice president, four levels above me in the food chain. So when my boss asked me to do this, my first reaction was to feel sick to my stomach. I regained my calm, though, because I knew from past experiences my manager would set me up to succeed.

My boss was available to review my work-in-progress so that I'd complete it successfully and stay on track. He let me do a practice presentation on him. He acted as both springboard and safety net.

It turned out that toll-free support was incredibly expensive, so the recommendation not to implement it was easy.

And when I ran the number to guess WordPerfect's phone costs, we predicted they'd have to stop the service soon. They did.

So I survived my presentation, thanked my manager, and was able to take on the next assignment with more confidence and use less of his time.

Here are some suggestions based on how Microsoft managers mentor their teams:

- Show your team HOW you make decisions—take them through your thought process.
- Help them prepare for a presentation or let them help you prepare for one of yours.
- Give assignments that will expose them to upper management—be around to answer questions along the way.
- Send them to a meeting in your place. They'll feel great about being chosen to go.
- Give them new responsibilities that will make them work on their weaknesses.
- Let them spend a day with one of your colleagues in another division or functional area to see what goes on over there.
- Suggest and give them the time to take continuing education classes.
- Bring them to some higher-level meetings, if only just to watch.
- Arrange team lunches with upper-level managers.
- Lead by example.

L E S S O N

3

FRIEND VS. BOSS

It's hard to strike the right balance between being liked and being respected. If you're too friendly with your group and socialize with them, it may be hard for you to give unpleasant feedback. If you're too aloof, they may be afraid to approach you with questions and problems. " 'Friendly' is great, but 'friend' may be over the line," one manager told me.

I had a very nice boss. He was so nice he never wanted to hurt anyone's feelings. So he soft-pedaled his criticism. He downplayed it so well, in fact, that no one knew when they were being told to improve something. His feedback was so sugarcoated, the whole team thought they were stars. This, of course, caused a problem when he did their reviews and gave them less-than-stellar scores.

Being friends with just one of your employees can cause even more problems. In a group working near me, one of the managers, Jack, became good friends with Teddy, one of his employees, when they started carpooling to work together. Soon they were dropping by each other's offices or grabbing a quick lunch together. They started socializing outside of work; their wives became friends; inside jokes started developing between them.

The rest of the team started to feel excluded. Why didn't the boss stop by their office? What were those two always laughing over? In meetings they wondered if their boss was favoring Teddy's ideas just because the two were friends. Was Jack really objective anymore? This friendship started to undermine Jack's credibility, and the team started to lose respect for him. A few months later, Teddy was promoted. But people wondered if he deserved it or if Jack had bestowed it on him.

The team started to fall apart, missing deadlines, speaking critically of Jack and the team morale. It got so bad that Jack was eventually demoted and left the company. This is an extreme example, but favoritism in this case stalled one man's career.

▼   SUGARCOATING YOUR MESSAGE   ▲

The following E-mail message spoofs managers who can't tell it like it is.

TO:	Project Review Group
FROM:	Dean Hachamovitch
RE:	Suggestions for official Project Review terminology

INSTEAD OF "JOE WAS A DOPE":
   The team had a quality problem in certain areas.
   Certain members of my team demanded structured
      tasks.
   This team member's skills lie elsewhere.

INSTEAD OF "IT WAS JOE'S FAULT":
   Our Quality Assurance process was lacking.
   Our communications channels failed.
   Certain gears didn't engage.

INSTEAD OF "JOE WAS DISORGANIZED":
   . . . had little to no structure.
   . . . not ready for prime time.

INSTEAD OF "JOE HAS LEFT MICROSOFT TO SEEK OTHER OPPORTUNITIES":
   We lost a resource.
   This should be less of a problem in the future.

➡   **⬇**

LESSON

4

NO SURPRISES AT REVIEW TIME

Feedback along the way is easier to give, hear, and take action on, than one-time feedback at review time. If your employees are making mistakes, let them know when they do it. Help them make course corrections along the way. They'll know where they stand with you. And their year-end review won't be a shock.

When an employee goes into a review saying, "I have no idea what my score is going to be," it means their manager is doing a poor job.

Making sure everyone is prepared for a review includes informing your own boss as well. At Microsoft employees are scored on a forced curve (a third of the people at a given level must get a certain score). Because only one third of the people are really in the top third, this works most of the time. However, there can be glitches. If your star doesn't get a top rating, he or she may be furious. This person's raise and bonus won't be great, and he or she may start thinking it's time for a different job.

Kathleen Schoenfelder, a general manager, has a great track record of getting her group the right scores. For the six months prior to review time, she keeps her boss informed about her team, including the areas they were responsible for, their kudos and screw-ups, and their strengths and areas where she is helping them to improve. So for Kathleen, the scores she submitted to her boss for her team were usually rubber-stamped. Her boss knew their work well. Another advantage of letting your boss know how the team is doing is that they may actually be able to help with your problem players. Perhaps your boss has faced a similar situation—an employee consistently not meeting deadlines or not communicating—and can give advice.

WHAT YOUR PERFORMANCE REVIEW SAYS . . . AND WHAT IT REALLY MEANS

(From an E-mail forwarded around Microsoft.)

TO:	Windows Group Managers
FROM:	?
RE:	Some help for review writing.

If you mean: ''Ignores everyone.''
Then say: ''Excels in sustaining concentration while avoiding confrontations.''

If you mean: ''Doesn't mind spending someone else's money.''
Then say: ''Is willing to take calculated risks.''

If you mean: ''Complains a lot.''
Then say: ''Identifies major management problems.''

If you mean: ''Passes the buck well.''
Then say: ''Delegates responsibility effectively.''

If you mean: ''Conserves supplies and funds by never doing anything.''
Then say: ''Optimizes the use of available resources.''

—By Staff Sgt. Frank Hendricks, writer for the Fort Devens, Mass., ''Dispatch.''

LESSON

5

HIRE SMART AND DON'T RUSH

A great hire can take the weight of the world off your shoulders. A poor performer can weaken an entire team and create a time sink for you as you try to compensate for them and help them improve. So hold out. Look one year, three years, five years down the road and ask, "Can this candidate grow to the next levels? Will they be successful with a variety of responsibilities or just the ones in the current position?"

A manager needed to fill an international marketing job and was in a rush. Rather than taking the time to find a person with the right skill set, he offered the spot to someone from one of Microsoft's international subsidiaries that he had met once on a business trip. He figured she knew what it was like to work in a subsidiary, so she'd know what they needed from headquarters. Francesca, it turned out, was a terrible fit for a job that required smooth communication and tracking lots of details.

She was completely disorganized. Her voice mail and E-mail boxes both got so full they shut down. Rather than improving processes for communication, swiftly funneling what was needed back and forth, she stopped information dead in its tracks. The subsidiaries started sending information requests to her boss, since they never heard replies from Francesca.

A few months later the perfect candidate for the job became available. Unfortunately for all, Francesca's agreement was to work in that position for two years. In retrospect, her manager realized that had he taken the time up front to interview and hire a great candidate, he would have saved himself and the company a great deal of energy later on.

Managers at Microsoft go mostly for raw talent over specific experience. As Group Vice President Jeff Raikes put it, "I'd rather have a fast computer I'll spend time with and program to do a variety of things, than one that comes preprogrammed for one task." The head of Office programming, Ben Waldman, tells his group, "Is the person you're interviewing smarter than half our group? They need to be. We want to raise the median, not lower it!"

Here are a couple of lessons I learned about interviewing prospective employees at Microsoft:

- Give a "hill" interview. Most candidates are nervous, so start off with easy questions about their background and interests to get them comfortable and performing at their best. Move into the challenging part of the interview when they're warmed up. Give them your hardest questions. Then ease down at the end, so they can finish with some strong answers and feel confident going into their next interview.
- Test the candidates' thought process and problem-solving ability, not their specific knowledge. So what if they don't know how many Windows users there are in the world or how to use pivot tables in Excel? If they think logically and creatively, they can get the specifics along the way. Some managers pose scenarios with key information missing to see if the candidate will ask for the data or just move straight to a solution.
- Keep a set of interview questions that work for you— ones that bring out differences in the candidates' creativity, problem solving, intelligence, and so on. By using the same questions, you can establish benchmarks for candidates.

- After each interview at Microsoft, the interviewer sends an E-mail with their impressions of the candidate to the human-resources person who is arranging the day, as well as to the manager who is doing the hiring. All Microsoft interview mail starts off with the words "Hire" or "No Hire" and then goes to specific feedback. A marginal "Hire," someone who just barely make it, should be a "No Hire." Your candidates should leap over the bar you set for them, not just squeeze over. And if you say, "No Hire for our group but may be okay in another group," you're doing everyone a disservice. If they're not good enough for your team, don't stick another group with them.

L E S S O N

6   KEEP THE ATMOSPHERE FUN

Teams bond in the course of sharing experiences, whether they involve hard work or playtime. Fun builds camaraderie and morale. So take time out to loosen up every now and then, and make special events memorable.

Chief Financial Officer Frank Gaudette made each entrance at the annual company meeting a memorable event, once appearing to be fired from a cannon in superhero tights and on another occasion doing a John Belushi Blues Brothers imitation. Senior executives Steve Ballmer and Mike Maples "swam" across Lake Bill on the Microsoft campus as part of a United Way giving campaign, while other executives have lined up in a dunking booth. To get the sales force motivated to sell LAN Manager upgrades (a network product), marketer Mike Murray invented a program called GULP, exhorting the team to "sell more 'LAN Man' than Seven-Eleven sells Big Gulps."

The head of Office programming, Ben Waldman, needed his team to stay late on certain days of the week, so he gave a prize to the person who came up with the best name: he made working hard on a "Masochistic Monday" or a "Thermonuclear Thursday" a little more festive.

Pete Higgins, a group vice president, gave a talk to one thousand sales people in the persona of "Mister Rogers" at a national sales meeting. He wore a cardigan sweater, rode in on a tricycle, and changed from his shoes to his sneakers as the crowd roared. He delivered a good part of his speech in Rogers-esque fashion: "Marketshare. Can you say that, boys and girls? Mar-ket-share?" He got their attention, delivered his message, and garnered the highest marks of any session.

4 ALL I REALLY NEED TO KNOW ABOUT COMMUNICATION I LEARNED AT MICROSOFT

Communicating not only means getting your points across succinctly and successfully, it means listening to verify that the message was understood by your listeners. It also means understanding the appropriate way to influence and win others over to your views. Sometimes yelling works; other times, whispering is the attention getter. Knowing which tactic to use when separates the real communicators from the rest of the bunch.

WORDS

L E S S O N

1

YOUR STYLE

Go with your own style for presentations, meetings, negotiations, and as a manager. It's hard to make someone else's style work for any length of time, and in the end you probably won't be as effective with it as the person it really belongs to.

Microsoft executive vice president Steve Ballmer has a unique personality, an interesting communication style, and more energy than any five people combined. He gets super-excited over good events and bad. He yells things three times, pounding his fist into his other hand for emphasis on each repetition. He can get the entire Microsoft sales force pumped about an idea in one minute flat. A few Microsoft managers have noted Steve's success and tried to adopt his way of doing things, with ridiculous results. One fellow tried Steve's booming, hyper, repetitive presentation style at a big meeting. People thought he was joking and started to laugh.

If you do want to change your style, don't try it out on the first day of a new job. A group of MBAs, starting at Microsoft on the same day, had a lunch to meet some of the executives. Dave, an MBA from Stanford, got into a knock-down-drag-out argument with high-level managers over some marketing issue, shocking the whole table with his aggressive assault and temper. His peers got the impression he was unreason-able and slightly scary, so they stayed away from him for the next two years as they formed friendships and working relationships with each other. Well, it turned out that Dave had taken an "assertiveness training" class the week before he started at Microsoft and was trotting out his stuff. It took two somewhat lonely years for his peers to discover the real Dave, a reasonable, kind, mild-mannered guy!

LESSON

2

WHAT DID THAT QUESTION REALLY MEAN?

Freud said, "Sometimes a cigar is just a cigar." It's the same with questions. A question can be a straight-forward request for information. But a question can also be a suggestion, a reminder, a scolding, or a setup to make you look great. Take a moment to consider what someone is really asking for.

When Rich Tong, a vice president in the Windows NT group, asked, "Have you thought about X?" he really meant, "I think you've forgotten to consider X, which may be impor-tant, but I wanted to let you know this in a polite way."

When my boss Charlotte asked for "an update on the in-formation for Bill Gates," she wanted to remind me it was almost due.

Marketing Manager Susan Weeber once asked a question about the legal market in a meeting, knowing her team mem-ber had just done research on it, would give a great answer, and would gain credibility with new team members in the room he'd be working with.

3   DETAILS IMPLY TRUTH

Details imply truth, and numbers imply facts. Get specific to get believed, whether you're pitching an idea in a meeting, responding to a question, or trying to win an argument.

Before we knew much about PR, we'd respond to press questions with round numbers and vague answers. If the press called about a problem with Word, we'd call our phone support people, who could tell us how many people had called with the problem and how many more people were likely to be affected. Then we'd tell the press, "It's no big deal. Don't worry about it. If anyone has a problem, there's a fix available." The next day we'd be surprised to see an article about the problem.

Seeing this, we then tried to give the reporters more detailed information in an effort to convince them not to write the article. We'd get mind-numbing detail on facts and figures from our product-support folks so we could say, "We have had one hundred thirty-one calls on this problem out of the last five thousand five hundred total calls. That's two-point-three-eight percent. The problem only occurs with a certain bios which only eleven percent of all PC users around the world have. Of those users, forty-two percent probably use Word, and since only nine percent of Word users use this feature, according to our last research study, we don't expect to get many more calls. For anyone that calls, there is a patch available on the Microsoft Web site or we will mail it out free."

From that barrage of detailed and ultimately boring information, the reporters saw there wasn't much of a story to tell and they'd usually drop it.

4

PRESENTING VS. SELLING

There are times to sell, sell, sell. And then there are times to just plain present—including the pros and cons, providing a balanced view, and showing the warts—to get the right decision made.

When marketer Steve Bridgeland shows off his product at a software trade show in five-minute spurts, he's hyper, he's enthusiastic, he gushes over the product. He usually brings the house down. His job isn't to tell customers everything, just to tell them enough to get them to consider buying.

In contrast, when he presents a proposal at work, he's more measured and self-critical. He wants the best decision made for his product, so he presents the facts in a clear, impartial way. He lays out all the pros and cons. He details the risks and competitive threats. He pokes holes in his own arguments in an effort to try to present all sides. And his audience doesn't automatically go into "push back" mode, challenging his every assumption, as they might if they felt he was just trying to sell them on his idea.

LESSON

5

PRAISE PUBLICLY, CHASTISE PRIVATELY

It's great to hear, "Thanks, that was great work." It's even better when your boss hears it too! If you think a good thought about someone's work, share it with lots of folks. But if someone botches an assignment, blunders in a meeting, or is failing in their job, let them know in private.

Take time out to appreciate what goes on around you. On one great Friday at work, a colleague backed me up in a meeting, the corporate librarian went above and beyond the call of duty to get me some urgent information quickly, and my assistant spent twenty minutes on hold to get me an earlier flight home from the following week's business trip. I thanked them all via E-mail and where appropriate CC'd their manager.

Doing the opposite is almost always appropriate when someone makes a mistake. Don't chastise publicly. One Microsoftie, Karen, would often cut people off in meetings. She'd respond to what they were saying before they finished saying it. She'd shoot down ideas in mid-explanation. A few times her boss said, "Karen, just shut up for a minute and let them finish!" This worked temporarily, but it was definitely the wrong approach. Karen thought it undermined her in the meeting and reinforced her "hard to work with" reputation. It also destroyed the unified front she liked to have with her boss in meetings. She became defensive, so the message didn't really sink in.

Finally, her boss spoke to her privately in a calm moment

saying, "You're so focused on the issue at hand that you don't realize your style is affecting people's reaction to you. They feel assaulted, rather than listened to, so they become combative or clam up. Take the time to sit back and listen. Think for a minute, a whole minute, then speak up." In this calmer setting, alone with her boss, Karen got the message, and her meeting behavior subsequently improved. Chastising privately can help keep the person focused on your message, rather than their embarrassment in front of a group.

L E S S O N

6 GIVE ACTIONABLE FEEDBACK

Whether you are reviewing an employee's work, an ad concept from an agency, or a new staffing plan, your feedback needs to be clear, specific, and actionable.

During a performance review, my friend's boss told him, "You need to be more strategic." What did that mean, my friend asked. What should he do to be more strategic? Could his boss give examples of times he should have been more strategic than he was? His boss had a hard time explaining it, so my friend concluded it was just an excuse for not giving him a promotion, and he didn't change the way he worked.

He kept the same job, working on Microsoft's channel (in-store) planning, but got a new boss. This one reviewed his work and told him, "You need to give me more than a list of stores where our product will be carried. Look at the bigger picture. You need to figure out the key customer issues; let me know what they are and how we can address them. You need to understand our competitors' in-store plans and goals. What are their tactics and how do they map to the goals? What should our plan be in response?"

"Ah ha," my friend thought, "that's what 'be more strategic' means." This time the feedback he received was clear, specific, and actionable, so he could really use it.

LESSON

7

THERE'S ALWAYS ONE MORE PERSON WHO NEEDS TO KNOW

Whether you're communicating something by E-mail, memo, or via a meeting, there's usually someone you've forgotten to include. So take a minute to think about everyone who has a stake in it, and don't leave anyone out.

The Word, Excel, and Office teams wanted to unify their packaging so customers could tell the programs worked together and were part of a set. To do this, they chose to put a very distinctive looking vertical black band at the left on the front of the box. The product managers, creative-services folks, sales force, manufacturing, and software stores were all informed of this new look, and hundreds of thousands of boxes were printed. Soon however, a panicked call came from the Italian subsidiary. A black band around an envelope was a symbol for funerals and death in Italy. The foreign subsidiaries hadn't been consulted or informed early enough on the new box. They suffered great embarrassment in front of their customers.

International issues are notoriously sticky. The parliament of India banned the sale of Windows 95 when it was discovered that a map showing time zones did not accurately reflect the India-Pakistan border. Eventually a host of other problems also cropped up around this map, and it was removed from the product entirely.

Taking the time to think through who will care about your decision, findings, or output can really reduce headaches and hassle later.

LESSON

8

WHY PUBLISH?

Send out a memo if it is the most efficient way of passing along information, will save someone from duplicating the work you just did, or sometimes just to let people know what you are doing.

When I was working in the Consumer Division, part of my job entailed evaluating proposals from people outside the company who wanted to create a new CD-ROM title with Microsoft. Similar to would-be authors pitching a book to a publishing house, they'd send in a proposal that included their idea, target market, expertise on the subject matter and technology, sales projections, and so on.

Out of each one hundred proposals, approximately five would make it by me to our editorial board, which consisted of people with a variety of expertise. This group would discuss each proposal and decide if we should recommend it for funding.

To keep the board in the loop on the ninety-five rejects, I sent out a monthly memo that listed the proposals I had turned down, a short description of each, and the reason I rejected it. This saved them from having to read all the proposals themselves, let them object if they wanted one of the rejects brought before the board, kept them abreast of the ideas flowing in from the marketplace, and kept everyone on the same page as far as evaluation criteria went.

Memos can be used to share practices that work well and probably will work well with others. Microsoft product teams, whether they are in marketing, testing, or programming, often face similar problems and processes. If you've found a better way to solve or do things, send it around.

This may sound crass or political, but sometimes it's good to publish just to let people know what you're up to. Two entry-level marketers had similar jobs. Both excelled at their tasks, but one sent out memos stating her project's status and the new things she was doing; the other didn't. Guess who was given additional opportunities because her group all knew the work she was capable of?

Every company and industry has insider language, abundantly stocked with acronyms. The following E-mail message from an employee suggests some new variations on Microsoft's own OLE—Object Linking and Embedding. (For the technically curious, Object Linking and Embedding lets users put output from one piece of software into another, such as putting a picture into a word-processing document. This, however, has little to do with the spoof definitions below.)

TO:	Office Marketing Team
FROM:	Joan Morse
RE:	Important New Acronyms

Key point: pronounce OLE as ''oh-lay,'' and then read along . . .

OLE—Microsoft's object-linking and embedding technology.

OBE—Microsoft's sadism and masochism technology.

OJE—Microsoft's technology, it's not just for breakfast any longer.

OME—Microsoft's begging technology (as in, ''OME I please have more stock options, please?''). Also known as WFW, or Whining for Windows.

OKE—Microsoft's pretty agreeable, get-along-with-everyone technology.

OGE—Microsoft's open-hiring-policy technology for people with same-sex partners.

OHE—Microsoft's workgroup/meeting technology, as in, ''OHE, one more thing.''

OSE—Microsoft's national anthem technology.

ONE—Microsoft's pig Latin for Windows—for those of you who have forgotten your sixth-grade pig Latin, translated, ''o-nay'' means ''no.''

OPE—a new add-in for MS Money—provides small businesses with payment-collection capabilities.

OTE—Microsoft's Little Rascals' technology (developed in the Consumer Division).

OYE—what we say when another software maker signs up for OLE.

OLE3—Microsoft's kinky new mating technology.

OyVE—Microsoft's ''it's all right, we'll stay here alone in the dark'' technology.

➡ ⬇

MEETINGS

LESSON

1

DO YOU REALLY NEED TO GO TO THE MEETING? AND ONCE THERE, MUST YOU STAY?

What's the purpose of the meeting? Can you get the same thing done in less time via E-mail or phone? Being hardheaded about your time can save you lots of it.

General Manager Charlotte Guyman gets "invited" to a variety of meetings. But she doesn't go to a lot of them. She always asks the organizer, "Why do I need to be there? What is the purpose of the meeting? Am I the best one to go, or can I send someone from my team?"

If she goes to a meeting, she asks for any prereading or other work she needs to do before the meeting. She also refuses to go to any meeting that is without an agenda, making sure the organizer is indeed organized. This way, Charlotte cuts out thirty to forty percent of her meetings, often accomplishing the same thing by phone, E-mail, or by sending a team member in her stead. She also makes it home (most nights!) to have dinner with her kids.

Once you get to a meeting, you may realize it's not about what you thought or that you're the wrong person to be there. Don't be shy about saying, "Why are we having this meeting?" or "Do I really need to be here?" In some cases you may want to cancel the meeting entirely! I attended a meeting to discuss staffing for the following year. The woman assigned to present a finished staffing plan for approval seemed to be working on the plan in the meeting. The attendees said, "Why don't we postpone this meeting until tomorrow, when the plan is done?" The staffing head was embarrassed but showed up the next day with a completed plan.

When you go to a meeting, give it your full attention. A product manager who imagined himself to be the model of efficiency brought his laptop computer to every meeting. If the topics didn't pertain to him, he'd read his E-mail. He also liked to type up the action items from the meeting and E-mail them so they'd beat the attendees back to their desks. The annoying clicking of his keys and his apparent inattention to the meeting (his head was always down in his screen) made him seem not to care about what was being said, and he was gradually included in fewer meetings and eventually fell out of the communication loop. So, even though it's the electronic age, preserve your value at these gatherings by doing things the old-fashioned way with paper, pencil, and eye contact.

L E S S O N

2

DISCUSS THE ANALYSIS, DON'T PRESENT THE DATA

Everyone can read data, findings, or a report before they get to the meeting. Instead of droning through detailed information, take advantage of the brainpower in the room to discuss, solve, or brainstorm.

Every six months, the Consumer Division receives an enormous amount of sales data, customer feedback, and market information. In the past, the researchers would compile seventy-five-slide presentations, gathering the top managers in the room to present the results and the researchers' conclusions. Recently though, the researchers have started to send the data and analysis around in advance so the gathered managers can read it before the meeting and use their time together to flag issues, questions, and strategic implications. Two hours of detailed data delivery has turned into two hours of strategic discussion among the top managers. The results from this have included pricing changes, assignments to track competitors, and staff reorganizations to meet market changes.

LESSON

3

SOLVE CONTROVERSIAL ISSUES IN ADVANCE

Addressing controversial issues in advance can prevent public arguments that can defocus the meeting.

The Word team was preparing for their "program review," a review of their product's plans and progress with Bill Gates. The project head had decided to eliminate an entire area of software features and redeploy the people working on it to another area of the product. Rather than springing this major change on Bill during the meeting, the manager told him in advance. Bill reacted angrily. He completely disagreed with the decision. But the manager persevered, explaining their reasons further, and a compromise was worked out. The team's presentation later that week went smoothly, there were no surprises, and the issue didn't cause a ripple.

In contrast, a young manager presenting her three-year plans to the senior management of her division caused a complete ruckus with just her first point—dropping her product's price. The attendees argued so vehemently for so long that she never made it to her second point, and she was later chastised for not letting people know in advance that the issue was going to be raised.

L E S S O N

4

RUNNING THE MEETING

A good meeting can solve problems, disseminate information, bring disparate parties together, and give birth to new ideas. A bad meeting can waste time, annoy the attendees, and leave any situation in worse shape.

Try the following if you're running a meeting:

- Start on time; stay on time. When you start a meeting of ten people just ten minutes late, you've just wasted one hundred minutes of company time. If you get a reputation for starting meetings on time, people will more likely show up on the dot so they don't miss anything.
- Stick to the agenda/topic. Lots of meetings veer off course.
- Take notes, or ask someone else to take notes, so you can report what went on.
- Cut off windbags. Statements like, "So what you're saying is . . ." or "We should probably keep moving so we can cover everything," can politely interrupt diatribes.
- Encourage the silent ones.
- It's hard for people to fall asleep in small groups. The smaller the meeting, the harder it is for people to zone out or not participate.
- The last five minutes are crucial. Save time to summarize, assign action items, and agree on next steps.
- Do ruthless follow-up. Answer questions you promised to. Make sure people are doing their action items. Close open issues.

LESSON

5

ATTENDANCE TRICKS

Food, cool show-and-tell items, and a convenient time (not 6 PM Friday) are some of the tactics Microsofties use to make sure their meetings are well attended.

In the Kids and Games business unit, the last person to arrive at the meeting (if they came after the official start time) had to buy breakfast for the whole team the following week. In another group, the last person to arrive had the unpleasant task of taking notes, typing them up, and sending them around.

The head of the Office software group (three hundred people) would hold fifteen-minute team meetings once a month. People quickly realized that if they were late, they'd miss it entirely.

At each monthly meeting of one group that created computer games, the manager made sure to always show a sneak preview of a cool product under development. It would be first on the agenda to ensure the timely arrival of attendees. Using the opposite tactic, Bill Gates is saved for the end of the hours-long company meeting to entice people to stay.

A Consumer Division manager celebrated any birthdays or special events at the start of the meeting, so people felt it would be rude to the honoree to come in late, and didn't.

The Windows 95 launch meetings were held at the exact same time, in the same conference room, every week so no one could forget where they had to be or when. Food, a key motivator, was always served.

E-MAIL

LESSON

1

KNOW YOUR E-MAIL COMMANDS

E-mail is easy, it's fast, and you have a record of "conversations." It is also evil. It will control your every waking thought, consume vast amounts of your time, and can follow you no matter where you try to hide. Managing your E-mail and knowing proper E-mail etiquette are required skills today.

Does using the "r" command send the reply just to the sender or to everyone copied on the mail? What does "view session log" mean? Learn how your E-mail works, or prepare for some embarrassment.

A rising star was promoted to head up a business in Microsoft's Consumer Division. To celebrate, she went on a ski weekend with some girlfriends. The running joke of the weekend concerned the closet of one of their grandmothers, who, while single her whole life, at age eighty-five was discovered to have quite a collection of sex toys. Writing an E-mail to thank her friends for the nice weekend, the young star joked "Well, I guess I better clean all those sex toys out of my closet before I start my new job."

She hit the keys that she thought would send the message and then started composing her next E-mail, which was to the business unit, introducing herself to her new team of fifty marketers, programmers, and the like. Unfortunately, that last set of commands had interpolated her first E-mail into her second, and the whole business unit received both messages. Many of them stopped by her office to inquire if they could help their new boss with her cleaning.

2

LOOK CLOSELY AT THE RECIPIENT'S NAME YOU JUST TYPED

Careful with those flying fingers! Misspelled E-mail names have led to everything from memos evaporating into the great electronic black hole to discovered love affairs. There are stories at Microsoft that have taken on mythic proportions based on misspelled E-mail names.

A woman met a guy at a party. He was wearing an orange jumpsuit. The two hit it off. She sent a message to him the next day saying, "I'd like to see you again . . . in or out of that orange jumpsuit." She sent it to JonS instead of the fellow she had met, whose E-mail name was JonSt. JonS was Jon Shirley, the president of Microsoft. Luckily Jon Shirley had a sense of humor. Over the years he had received more than a few misaddressed missives. He forwarded it to JonSt, adding, "This is the best one yet."

One day, the general manager of a multi-hundred-million-dollar business received this simple E-mail declaration from someone she'd never met: "I just wanted to say, I love you very much." She replied, "I'm flattered, but assume you meant to send this to another Kathleen."

Another E-mail stumble happened when a midlevel Microsoftie manager was exploring some job transfer possibilities for himself. He composed a message to Linda, his colleague and confidante, saying, "I just don't think I could work for X. He is a complete suck-up." Linda had two associated E-mail names. One delivered mail to her directly and the other, ironically called "Linda Smith Direct," went to her direct reports, her team. Not paying close attention to his address line, the manager mistakenly sent this message to his friend's team of seven people. He followed up sheepishly with another E-mail stating, "If you'd like any more of my personal opinions on senior executives, just ask."

E-mail aliases (groups of people under one team name, such as Win95Mktg or SalesTeam) require even more digital vigilance!

One Father's Day, an employee wrote a long, heartfelt letter to his dad. Unfortunately, the Desktop Applications Division at Microsoft had the E-mail alias of DAD. It was a lovely letter, but not intended for the five hundred software developers, testers, and marketers who received it.

Someone in the Paris subsidiary once mistakenly asked the entire U.S. sales force to lunch in French. If you make this scale of blunder, you will feel compelled to send a note of apology. Don't do it! That's just one more piece of mail five hundred people don't need to see. You can safely assume they'll realize your message was a mistake.

Even the plain old Reply button needs to be used with caution. Once, at a trade show, a lovesick marketer borrowed his colleague's portable PC to send some E-mail to his honey back home. He lamented that he couldn't be with her for Valentine's Day and proceeded to describe all the things he would like to do to her and with her if he were home. She received the message and replied with exactly what she'd like to do back to him when they next met. Unfortunately, rather than type in her boyfriend's name, she hit the Reply button to send this, and it went to the young Romeo's colleague instead!

LESSON

3

E-MAIL HAS NO SOCIAL SKILLS

E-mail can be very terse. People jot down efficient little notes, requests, and commands that lack the social niceties of human-to-human interaction. You can't hear the sender's tone of voice, see their facial expressions, or watch their body language. Your quick note can sound like a demand. Even if you do the rest of your job with aplomb, getting a "nasty E-mailer" reputation can slow you down.

When your boss sends you the missive "Please stop by my office as soon as you can" you may not know whether you're going to get congratulated or read the riot act.

E-mails rarely start out with "Hey, how's it going?" as you might say if you stopped by someone's office. E-mails mostly just launch into their statement or request. So, think how the E-mail you're writing might get read. You may need to do more explaining over the wires ("Please stop by my office; I'd like to go over the agenda for the meeting") than you would face to face or over the phone, where the person can interrupt you or ask for clarification. And while those little keyboard smiley faces, :), or shocked expressions, :(), may look totally dumb, they can sometimes help get your meaning across.

One perfectly nice Microsoft salesperson wondered why his E-mail requests for materials, information, and support from headquarters took twice as long to get answered as those of his colleagues. It turned out that his E-mails, written in staccato bursts, were perceived as rude, demanding, and if they didn't look urgent, were put at the end of the queue.

LESSON

4

WATCH OUT FOR E-MAIL FORGERY

If it looks unbelievable, it just might be. E-mail pranks abound at Microsoft and offices around the world. If you don't want anyone sending fake mail that looks as though it's from you, turn off your E-mail when you leave the office.

E-mail can be faked. In the summer of 1989, a message that appeared to be from Microsoft president Jon Shirley went to every single employee of the company announcing layoffs. It sure looked authentic and caused a panicked buzz in the hallways, but it was the work of a hacker. Another prankster sent a message from the boss's terminal telling his team of seventy-five people to take the rest of the day off.

This kind of hacking doesn't seem to be too hard to do and can happen on a much smaller scale. One day a young marketer, Susan, told her friend Tara, "I can't believe what I just did! I walked into the cafeteria, got a cookie, then started talking to someone and walked out without paying. Whoops!" Later that afternoon, Susan received a long, serious E-mail from the "lunchroom director." She didn't know there **was** a lunchroom director. It stated, "At 12:30 PM today our staff witnessed you stealing an item of food from the cafeteria. Because this has been happening in the cafeteria more and more frequently, we must take steps, including notifying your boss."

Susan's face turned red and her palms started sweating as she sat reading the mail. The message went on in this fashion and not until it stated, "We ask you to refrain from eating chocolate for the next 2 weeks," did she realize it was a joke. One of Tara's friends, a programmer, had sent the mail.

▼ DON'T SEND THAT ANGRY E-MAIL—WAIT UNTIL YOU'VE CALMED DOWN ▲

(Excerpted from a piece of employee E-mail in 1985 to CEO Bill Gates and President Jon Shirley, who had just announced that the day the company moved to its new campus would be counted as an employee vacation day.)

TO:	BillG, JonS
FROM:	Name deleted!
RE:	Moving Day

Dear Jon,

I am quite happy to hear that the construction of the new campus is 60% complete. Here in Operating Systems, things have been going well for me, too; I am releasing my second network program this week.

I was really fascinated with the way you changed Presidents' Day. I didn't know that Microsoft had that sort of clout. When is Christmas this year? It wouldn't really matter to me, except that I have made plans for that weekend. Of course, the reimbursement for the deposit I placed on the hotel room is nothing to as profitable a company as Microsoft, so I'm sure that there are no hard feelings about that.

Not many companies with a balance sheet like ours would let the staff donate their holidays to help; I was flattered. Microsoft moved me across the country; the least I can do is move it across the county.

It took me a little while to figure out why you were being so nice and letting me help with the move. Then I realized that it was a matter of corporate image. Most companies, when they don't have work for people, lay them off. They say: "We don't have work for you. Come back next week." This is old hat, though. It has been done before. It's not in the forefront of technology, or the avant-garde of labor relations. Lee Iacocca has already written a book about it. Bruce Springsteen has already written a song about it. Microsoft is different. We are the cutting edge, the leaders in the field, the revolutionaries in corporate America.

We don't have layoffs, we have calendar reform. We say:

''We don't have work for you. That means tomorrow is the 4th of July, the day after that is Christmas, and then it's your personal holiday and then Labor Day. Come back next week.''

Calendar reform is new. It is exciting. It is different. I, for one, am proud to be working for Microsoft. If you call Mr. Springsteen, I'll start working on the song lyrics.

Sincerely,
(Name deleted)

5 ALL I REALLY NEED TO KNOW ABOUT MANAGING MY CAREER I LEARNED AT MICROSOFT

Sometimes you can get so wrapped up in the day-to-day demands of your job that you neglect your overall career—the old "forest for the trees" syndrome. It is important to be a success in your current position, but it's also critical to identify your goals and priorities and do all you can to achieve them. Think about what you want in the long run—don't just go blindly up the ranks, seeking that next promotion. Sometimes taking a lateral move to become more well-rounded (thinking two jobs ahead to where you'll end up next) is the smartest way to go. The person who cares most about your career is you (and maybe your mom), so don't shortchange yourself by not giving it the thought and energy it needs.

GETTING THE JOB YOU WANT

LESSON

1

KNOW YOURSELF BEFORE YOU CHOOSE YOUR JOB

Do you like to be at the center of the action? Do you need calm stability to perform at the top of your game? Do you crave intellectual provocation? Maybe a good boss is the most important factor for you. Figure it out before you make your next job change.

Sarah Leary is smart, young, and energetic. She was the country's top-ranked women's lacrosse goalie in college and brought that same intensity and focus on winning to Microsoft. She spent her first few years on the Word marketing team, helping grow the product into a billion-dollar business. It was a high-profile team with a big budget and lots of visibility.

She dove into her work at full speed, with great results, never afraid to take on risky projects or tight deadlines. She met each challenge and was rewarded with more tough assignments. She was chosen to show off Microsoft's Office product, bantering back and forth with TV star Jay Leno at the Windows 95 launch, which was beamed around the world by satellite.

After the launch, Sarah was given the chance to join the international marketing team. She agreed, envisioning trips to Europe and Asia, learning how to do business across different cultures. Heady stuff for someone just twenty-six years old. But the job took Sarah away from the center of the action. In fact, her main job now was just to communicate what was happening in her old group to the subsidiaries. That meant lots of E-mail. Lots of memos. Lots of planning. And all of it about work that others had done. She was bored to tears.

Sarah hated being on the outside. True she visited Russia and Europe. True she worked fewer hours and had fewer deadlines to meet. But she couldn't stand missing out on all the action. Four months later she asked to switch jobs again. She agreed to jump into the planning for a huge press presentation on a new area, "the Intranet," where she pulled all-nighters, cranked out volumes of work, and was happy again.

You may do best in a "smooth sailing" job. Maybe "choppy water" is your thing. Find the environment you like and go for a spot that offers you the best of that world.

LESSON

2

NO ONE CARES MORE ABOUT YOUR CAREER THAN YOU

Microsoft executive vice president Mike Maples always told us to manage our own careers because no one cares more about your success than you yourself. Whether it's finding a lateral move to broaden your skills or a group where you're the likely successor to the boss or getting some high-profile projects, don't be shy in asking for what you want.

After five years as an Excel programmer and then as head of Excel programming, Chris Peters posed an unusual request to his bosses.

"I'd like to take time off to get my MBA," he told them. "I definitely want to come back after the year or two, but I think I need to do this to become a general manager. I need to learn marketing. I want to be able to run a whole business, not just the technical side."

His bosses thought it over.

"We had no idea you wanted to be a general manager. We thought you just liked programming."

Chris explained some more about his interests, the things he thought he was good at, and where he needed to learn.

"What if you could learn those things on the job?" they asked. "If we made you a general manager now, would you still want to go to business school?"

"No," Chris replied.

So they made him the general manager of the Word business unit.

Point out what you're interested in and the opportunities are more likely to come.

LESSON

3

FIX YOUR SIGHTS ON THE CORRAL, NOT A FENCE POST

While it makes great sense to plan for the type of job, function, or level you're shooting for, don't get too hung up on that specific position or team.

Ben Waldman came to Microsoft in 1989 because he loved the Apple Macintosh and Microsoft was the leading software maker for the Mac. He started out as a programmer on Mac Excel and did indeed have a great time creating cool new software for Mac users.

Along the way, he was offered opportunities to work on other technologies and challenges. He took them. After a few years working on Mac Excel, he worked on some Windows issues. After that, his assignment focused on learning how novice users work with a PC and on human-computer interaction. He stayed open-minded about what might be fun, interesting, or challenging and worked his hardest on every new assignment. Just seven years later, still in his twenties, Ben was named head of development for Office Software, a multibillion-dollar part of Microsoft. He could never have achieved that level of responsibility if he had just stayed focused on Mac software or any other single technology or issue.

In contrast, an account manager from Microsoft's advertising agency joined Microsoft to work on brochures, direct-mail pieces, and other printed communication pieces. He was great at his job and became the manager of his team. However, he wouldn't consider any of the other opportunities coming his way that would have rounded out his experience in other areas of marketing. In a few years he reached the top of his specialized function. He loved Microsoft, but in order to continue growing in his chosen area, he had to leave and join another company.

If he had been more open-minded, found something he liked, he could have explored new areas, and stayed. Other employees have worked hard to get on a certain project run by a certain manager, but by the time they had the chance to switch jobs, the manager had changed, the team had reorganized, or the whole project had been canceled! So keep your eye on the bigger picture. Set your sights on a type of experience or position, but don't get too hung up on joining "that project." Stay unbiased. Opportunities may come along in areas you may not have even thought about.

L E S S O N

4   SOMETIMES THE FROG JOB CAN MAKE YOU A PRINCE

The most obvious, high-visibility, high-powered, "strategic" jobs may not always be the place to get the best experience. Look beyond the obvious in your job opportunities.

Moving from Word marketing to the CD-ROM area moved me out of the strategic, money-making nerve center of Microsoft. The total revenue of my twenty-five new CD-ROM products put together was less than ten percent of Word sales. But we were shipping a new title a month, so I got launch experience after launch experience (in Word, a new version was launched every eighteen months or so). I learned about a new customer segment and how to work with an emerging market. And when my boss switched jobs, I was put in charge of two hundred people—an opportunity I would've waited years for in Word!

My friend Stephanie was asked to create a newsletter when she switched to her new marketing job. She had done a newsletter in her entry-level job, and while she thought someone more junior would be more appropriate for the task, she decided to make the best of the situation. So she looked at the newsletter as a way of "building the Microsoft brand" rather than as a single piece of communication. Stephanie's first move was to take the group's existing newsletter, cut its cost in half, and reformat it to make it hipper. Then she commissioned research to find out about the people reading the newsletter, what they liked, wanted improved, and so on and made those changes. She found high-profile customers through this research and made them into spokespeople. The look and information of the newsletter was so improved it was also used in magazine advertisements. Stephanie was soon promoted to be the group's manager.

Sometimes it's sheer luck or great foresight that can launch you into the limelight. In the late 1980s J Allard was toiling away on an obscure network protocol called TCP/IP. It wasn't glamorous, but he felt it was going to be huge one day. He became the TCP/IP expert at Microsoft. That obscure protocol turned out to be the standard for the emerging Internet, and J, whose work is now incredibly important to the company, ended up featured in a *Business Week* article in 1996.

LESSON

5

FIGURE OUT WHAT YOU'D DO IN THE JOB—BEFORE THE INTERVIEW

Prepare. Prepare. Prepare. Your interviewer may ask you what you would do in the job if they gave it to you. So do some research and thinking before you walk into the interviewer's office.

Thinking about switching jobs, I asked the marketing manager of the Kids software group if I could talk to her informally about opportunities in her area. She agreed, and we set a time to meet.

When I walked into her office, I was immediately peppered with questions, "What do you think the biggest challenge is in this market? How would you improve our products? Would you spend your marketing dollars targeting parents or kids? We have a writing product and a drawing product—which would you try to bundle with new PCs? Why? What would you charge?"

I was shocked and completely unprepared, since I thought she'd be telling *me* about the area and its opportunities. Needless to say, I floundered around for an hour, and in the end they didn't want me to join their group. I was shell-shocked and dejected by the whole experience.

Some months later, I went to check out a group working on new CD-ROM products. The hiring manager told me these would be informal meetings, but this time I was going to be prepared. The night before my first meeting, I went out for dinner with a friend and went over lots of questions they might ask and how I might answer. I had a feeling they'd ask me to pick an area and go through a whole marketing plan for a CD-ROM in that area. I love to travel, so I imagined a Travel CD. My friend and I discussed its target market, its competition, its price, and the features it could offer on a computer that a book couldn't. We brainstormed ideas on marketing the new product.

Lo and behold, nearly everyone I met with asked me about CD-ROM marketing, and I used the Travel CD as an example. They asked me about customers, markets, competitors. I answered back with the things I had discussed over dinner the night before.

I got the job.

L E S S O N

6

BRING AMMUNITION TO YOUR JOB INTERVIEW

Whether it's your résumé, recommendations, past performance reviews, or examples of your work, give your interviewer the most compelling evidence of your talents.

You can begin amassing ammunition early. I had worked in Word for three years and knew I wanted a change. My review was coming up, so I asked my boss, "This review is going to be read by whoever is thinking of hiring me next. Can you make it really good?"

Responding to my request, he gave detailed information on what I had done and ended the review with a resounding recommendation. I brought that review with me when I met with a woman I wanted to work for. She could have gotten a copy of the review from Human Resoures, but I wanted to make sure she had it right after she spoke with me. I was hired.

Your interview ammunition can also be something you worked on. One memorable interviewee from the UCLA business school showed off his invention for businessmen— shirt garters attached to his socks. He was wearing them and pulled up his pant leg to demonstrate. Two years later another UCLA student wowed his female interviewer with a calendar full of bare-chested guys with guns he had put together called "Men of the Navy Seals."

Use your connections. I've asked my old boss to call someone who's thinking of hiring me to put in a good word. I gave another manager the names of people I worked with on different projects so she could call them if she liked.

LESSON

7

KEEP YOUR ONE-PAGE RÉSUMÉ UP TO DATE

Whether you're responding to a call from a headhunter or just switching jobs within your company, folks will appreciate a quick snapshot of your accomplishments.

Every six months, Microsofties write up their achievements for a performance review with their boss. When she tallies up her most recent accomplishments, my friend Katherine also updates her résumé. "As long as I'm thinking about what I've done, I might as well add it to my one-pager," she says.

This practice has served her well. By keeping a résumé on file, Katherine has been able to respond immediately to job opportunities. She also uses the résumé to review her experiences before an interview or returning a headhunter's call. Let's face it, who really remembers the major accomplishments from his or her job five years back? But that may be just the thing that puts you ahead of other candidates.

LESSON

8   DECIDE THE THREE MESSAGES OR ATTRIBUTES YOU WANT TO CONVEY

No matter what job interview questions you get asked, no matter what random direction your interviewer takes in his or her approach, you can get your message across.

My friend Judy went in for a job interview. To prepare herself, she had learned about the job and decided which of her strengths and experiences fit the needs of the position. She decided her leadership skills, creativity, and ability to get things done were the key attributes in this case and thought of strong examples of each that were related to the new job at hand. She was determined to get this information across in the interview.

Unfortunately, Judy's interviewer began asking her just about every sort of question except one that would allow her to bring up the things she wanted. Judy watched the minutes slipping by on the clock above her interviewer's head an finally jumped in with, "We haven't really touched on my retail experience, and I think it's important to the job because . . ." and proceeded to lay out the points she wanted to make.

Judy then followed that up with, "Do you have any concerns about me as a candidate that I might be able to address?" The interviewer thought a moment and said, "Well, you don't seem to have international experience, and this job does deal with our subsidiaries from time to time." Judy responded with her experience as an exchange student and the foreign travel she had done. But if she had never asked, the interviewer might never have brought up the international aspect of the job and just noted himself that Judy had no experience in that area. At the end of the interview, Judy said, "To sum up . . ." and succinctly restated the strengths and experience she would bring to the position.

By knowing what she wanted to say and finding ways of saying it—"We haven't touched on . . . ," "Do you have any concerns . . . ," and "To sum up . . ."—Judy was able to control the outcome of the interview much better and did get the job.

LESSON

9

"IF YOU WERE A SMALL ANIMAL, HOW SMALL WOULD YOU BE?"

If you've got your answers to the most common interview questions down in a concise, compelling way, you'll have more latitude to freelance on the more far-out queries.

The above title points out the sheer absurdity of some interview questions. And while some are truly on the fringe, some are standard and expected. Prepare in advance for the following questions. Since you know these questions are coming, it's worth taking the time to prepare for them rather than thinking on your feet.

• What are your strengths and weaknesses?

- Give me an example of
  your leadership
  your creativity
  your problem solving
  how your experience relates to this job
  a time you had to overcome great odds
  a well-marketed product and why you think it's well marketed
  a tough business problem you solved

When you get a far-out question, don't lose your composure. Take a minute to think about it. Silence is okay in the interview room.

Here are a few of the stranger questions:

- How many times does the average person use the word "the" in a day?
- Why are CDs the size they are?
- How many gas stations are there in the U.S.?

These are not a test of your trivia knowledge, but of your deductive reasoning and your composure. Break down your answer and think out loud so your tormentor—I mean interviewer—can hear your thought process.

For example, in the gas station question, you might start out with, "Well, there are two hundred and sixty million people in the U.S., one hundred million households. Of those, probably X percent have two cars, Y percent have one car, and rest don't own a car. If they fill up the tank once every two weeks, . . . ," and so on. You don't have to be superdetailed, precise, or know the driving habits of America; you just need to stay calm and work through it.

Some questions sound completely unrelated to the job you're going after, but think again. Software designers are asked to describe the perfect TV remote control to see how they break down the problem, how simple or complex they make the solution, and if that solution solves customer needs. These are the same qualities they'll need to use when they design software. A marketer may get asked, "If you were a product, how would you position yourself?" A candidate for a sales job may get handed a pencil and told, "Sell me this pencil."

You may get questions about things going on in the job you're applying for. At Microsoft that may be "What do you think are the pros and cons of selling software over the Internet?" or "If you had one hundred copies of Word to donate, would you give it to schools or libraries?" Just work through the answer out loud, pointing out where you don't know the industry or data, or other information you may need. Again, this isn't a test of your exact knowledge of the company's business. It's a problem-solving or idea-generation exercise. Sometimes data is left out of the question on purpose to see if you'll ask for it.

STAYING ON TRACK

L E S S O N

1

A CAREER IS A LONG TIME

Don't get hung up if you miss out on this year's promotion, your friend is making more money in the same job, or you didn't get the transfer you wanted. You may work for fifty years. Keep doing your best and it will all likely balance out.

"For every ten years you spend here, you're going to have to forgive us for three of them." That's how a senior manager explained to a younger manager why she didn't get the new job she wanted. Each person has their own career needs. But there are also the company's needs. And, there are things happening outside, such as economic trends, competitor's actions, or new technologies, that can affect the organization. The planets won't always align for you.

So, if you can't get what you want right away, your best bet is to do top work on whatever they give you. A talented product manager who worked for me agreed to take on lots of detailed, excruciating, eye-crossing financial reporting—work he hated doing—because he was the best one to do it. He did it with all his energy, he did a great job, and I know he hated almost every minute of it. I recognized his efforts and rewarded him for it. Knowing he wanted management experience more than anything, I assigned him our group's summer interns, choosing him over another, equally qualified team member.

A career might span fifty years. You can't always be on the fast track. You may need a break, have family obligations, or just want a change of pace every few years. This happens in a variety of ways at Microsoft, and the great thing is that people are allowed to step off the fast track and no one bats an eye. They're also allowed to jump back on it.

When a successful marketing manager of a major business left to go work on nascent baseball and basketball CD-ROMs, people said, "What a cool job. Sounds fun!" They didn't say, "What's wrong with his career? What does he think he's doing?" After a year and a half of meetings with the NBA, tickets to all-star games, and generally living the ultimate sports fan's fantasy, the manager returned refreshed, to a more strategic high-pressure business area.

Another manager traded in his job in charge of three hundred people for one on a team of thirty working on a new product where he'd have to write computer code. He had decided he wanted to learn about the Internet, wanted a break from being an administrator to return to his more technical roots, and looked forward to this change of pace. Other people have "taken a year off," literally leaving the company to travel and pursue hobbies, only to return twelve months later and pick up where they left off.

L E S S O N

2

HAVE YOUR OWN PERSONAL BOARD OF DIRECTORS

Find three or four people senior to you in the company who will be honest about how you're doing and advise you on your next move. Make them your informal guidance counselors and career advisers. They may point out your Achilles' heel or find you new job opportunities.

A friend of mine agonized over whether to stay in marketing and be promoted or to move to another functional area where he'd learn a new part of the business but have to stay at his same job level for another two years. The promotion was obviously very enticing.

He asked his "personal board of directors" for their advice. The first, his old boss, knew his work very well. She saw he was a bright, capable guy. She told him that early in his career, he should broaden his experience by taking the lateral move into the other department. While not as ego-gratifying as a promotion, he'd be better off in the long run by gaining a new area of expertise. His next mentor knew of an upcoming reorganization in the marketing department. She didn't tell him this information, which was highly confidential, but subtly steered him to the new department. His last mentor had worked extensively with the new department and could recommend it highly as a place to learn. Each of my friend's "personal board of directors" gave him individual input based on their experience with the company and with my friend. He took the lateral move and continues to do well at Microsoft today.

Your board of directors may also be able to help you beef up in specific professional areas. Break your job down into the skills it requires for success. Maybe it's negotiating, selling ideas, or rallying the troops. Ask your board of directors who around the company really embodies success in that skill so you can benchmark your actions versus theirs, or just learn by watching them.

L E S S O N

3

THE 360-DEGREE REVIEW

In a 360-degree review, you're examined from all sides. Your boss, your peers, and the folks that work for you fill out anonymous forms commenting on your strengths and areas for improvement. It's kind of scary to be under that kind of microscope, but if you can bear it, it's a great tool to find out how people perceive you at work.

There are firms that will help you do an official 360-degree review. Or you can just create your own forms and hand them out. As long as the forms can be filled out and submitted anonymously, you'll likely get some eye-opening and valid feedback.

A superstar rising through the ranks knew that her boss considered her to be smart, incredibly organized, and very efficient. But when she did the 360-degree review, she discovered an impresssion she had never imagined. A side effect of her being superefficient was that her peers considered her cold and unfriendly. And the people who worked for her felt intimidated when she spoke to them in her clipped, organized way. They felt she was unapproachable, so they didn't come to her with problems and ideas as often as they might have.

The star talked with some friends to try to figure out how to "be a real person," as she called it, as well as a high performer. She put their advice to work. Rather than jumping into a meeting's agenda, she'd take time to chat beforehand. In casual conversations, she let people know more about herself, talking about her husband or house remodeling. She started walking down different sets of hallways on the way to meetings and stopping by various people's offices to say hi. As she warmed up to people, they warmed up to her. Her peers invited her to lunch more often. Her team came to her when problems were brewing to get her feedback, rather than after they had unsuccessfully tried to solve them themselves (they had been afraid to do this before). Even her boss took her into her confidence more often. Although this transition was tough for a few months, the star ended up happier, with a closer working relationship with those around her.

LESSON

4

THINK TWO JOBS AHEAD

That new job looks fun, but is the group set up to succeed? A promotion sounds enticing, but is it really going to take you where you want to go in the long run? What's going to happen when you want to move on?

My boss Ron used to say, "Don't think about what your next job will be, think about where that job is going to get you." Do you want to be a specialist or generalist? Which job will take you down that path? Say you want to run your own company five years down the line. What are the jobs that will best prepare you for that? It's hard to escape the peer pressure to take the most prestigious promotion you can get your claws into, but keep your eye on the long-term goal and prepare yourself to meet it.

My friend Alex had lots of PR and advertising experience, but he knew that his best shot at becoming a general manager at Microsoft was to get "more technical" and learn how the products are created, not just how they're marketed. So he took a job that sort of scared him (what were all those bits and bytes people were talking about?) and wasn't as fun and glamorous as his old duties, but really forced him to learn the side of Microsoft's business he had never experienced. It was grueling, it made him uncomfortable, he almost jumped ship and went back to marketing two or three times, but in the end he persevered, struggling up the learning curve. At the end of two years, he looked back and realized he had gained a whole new skill set. Later on, he was given the opportunity to manage a group that included both marketing and technical folks—his managers saw he could now add value to both sides.

That said, don't go totally overboard and take a job you'll hate and do poorly, just to get to the next place. Often, just having a track record of success will keep your career on the move. Jeff Raikes (now a part of Microsoft's Office of the President) was put in charge of the sales force despite the fact he had never been a salesman or ever worked in the sales division. His skills and successes in previous positions made his manager (Bill Gates) decide he was the best candidate for the job.

L E S S O N

5

KEEP IT IN PERSPECTIVE

A mistake is not the kiss of death. If you keep it in perspective, you'll be able to recover quickly, learn from the mistake, and move on.

When someone would send out incorrect information to the sales force, give a bad quote to the press, or miss a deadline, Mac Word product manager Leslie Koch would tell them, "Don't worry, no small children will die." That may sound strange, but it always let us keep our mistakes in perspective. Our mistakes could be managed, fixed, and wouldn't really have any serious consequences. Where did she get this perspective? Leslie had previously worked for

New York City's Child Welfare Agency, where indeed, if she screwed up, a child might die. So the worst things we could do—lose money, miss opportunities—were things to be avoided, but in the end they were just things, not people.

Leslie also used to march down the halls at 10 PM when we were all still at our desks and demand, "Is this our youth? Is this how we want to spend our youth?" encouraging us all to go home.

DO MICROSOFTIES REALLY WORK THAT HARD?

(From an E-mail message sent around the company.)

TO:	Susan Weeber
FROM:	Stephanie Libresco
RE:	Security Breach

Heard this one today . . .

A Microsoft security guard caught two non-Microsoft employees playing volleyball on our campus volleyball court and asked them to leave the premises.

When asked by a fellow employee how he knew that the two were not Microsoft employees, the guard replied:

"They had tans."

L E S S O N

6

THERE IS NO "ENEMY WITHIN"

Sometimes, interoffice rivalries can get ugly and get in the way of doing business.

It's easy to get embroiled in group-dynamic politics. At Microsoft a few years ago, two groups of marketers were battling over budget and decision-making power. They fought over spending, communication, customer contacts, you name it. Tempers flared. Nasty E-mails abounded. People started making decisions for the good of their fiefdom, rather than doing what was best for the business.

Finally, one manager said, "We really need to compete against Lotus, WordPerfect, and Novell, not building nine." This statement was so simple and made so much sense that it spread quickly. People repeated it throughout the group. The teams sat down together, and slowly, over the next few months, things got less rocky and they joined forces to win customers.

LESSON

7

TEN WAYS TO BALANCE WORK AND LIFE

Actually, most Microsofties don't balance their work with their outside life. Microsoft consumes all the time and energy you'll give it. But here are a few ways I've seen my coworkers give the balance thing a try.

1.

Have an ongoing midweek date night with your significant other.

2.

Meet a friend at the gym. You're less likely to skip the workout if you know someone's waiting there for you.

3.

Sign up to help at a charity event or be on a board.

4.

Take a night class in something completely unrelated to your job, for example, ceramics, Japanese, or yoga.

5.

Go home at six, eat dinner with your family, put the kids to bed, and THEN do your E-mail.

6.

Get season tickets to the symphony or theater. You'd feel so guilty if you wasted the money that you're sure not to miss a performance.

7.

Pick two nights a week to leave at 6 PM. Stay as late as you need to the other three nights. This works better if you're single.

8.

Never schedule a meeting before 8 AM or after 5 PM. And not at all on a weekend.

9.

Plan lots of weekend trips. Hire someone to do the errands you'll be skipping.

10.

Microsofties can think of only nine ways (just kidding).